THE PENGUIN CLASSICS

FOUNDER EDITOR (1944–64): E. V. RIEU

HENRIK IBSEN was born at Skien, Norway, in 1828. His family went bankrupt when he was a child, and he struggled with poverty for many years. His first ambition was medicine, but he abandoned this to write and to work in the theatre. Of his early verse plays, *The Vikings at Helgeland* is now best remembered. In the year of its publication (1858) he married Susannah Thoresen, a pastor's daughter.

A scholarship enabled Ibsen to travel to Rome in 1864. In Italy he wrote *Brand* (1866), which earned him a state pension, and *Peer Gynt* (1867), for which Grieg later wrote the incidental music. These plays established his reputation. Apart from two short visits to Norway, he lived in Italy and Germany until 1891.

From *The League of Youth* (1869) onwards, Ibsen renounced poetry and wrote prose drama. Though a timid man, he supported in his plays many crucial causes of his day, such as the emancipation of women. Plays like *Ghosts* (1881) and *A Doll's House* (1879) caused critical uproar. Other plays included *The Pillars of the Community*, *The Wild Duck*, *The Lady From the Sea*, *Hedda Gabler*, *The Master Builder*, *John Gabriel Borkmann* and *When We Dead Wake*.

Towards the end of his life Ibsen, one of the world's greatest dramatists, suffered strokes which destroyed his memory for words and even the alphabet. He died in 1906 in Kristiania (now Oslo).

PETER WATTS was born in 1900 and went to school in Canada. He originally trained as a doctor at Cambridge and St Thomas's Hospital, but then turned to journalism and the theatre. In the twenties he stage-managed the Old Vic for eight years. He then travelled about Europe and the Middle East and after a period as a literary agent and then as a wine merchant he returned to the theatre in 1938 as a producer. When the theatres closed at the beginning of the war, he went to the Admiralty as a King's Courier, but left in 1941 when the BBC offered him a post as a drama producer. He remained with them for nearly twenty years, working both in radio and television. He produced most of his translations of Ibsen and Strindberg on the Third Programme. During his retirement, he lived by the sea in Cornwall. He died in 1972.

*Henrik Ibsen*

# PEER GYNT
## A DRAMATIC POEM

TRANSLATED WITH AN
INTRODUCTION BY
PETER WATTS

PENGUIN BOOKS

Penguin Books Ltd, Harmondsworth, Middlesex, England
Penguin Books, 625 Madison Avenue, New York, New York 10022, U.S.A.
Penguin Books Australia Ltd, Ringwood, Victoria, Australia
Penguin Books Canada Ltd, 2801 John Street, Markham,
Ontario, Canada L3R 1B4
Penguin Books (N.Z.) Ltd,
182-190 Wairau Road, Auckland 10, New Zealand

—

This translation first published 1966
Reprinted (with minor revisions) 1970
Reprinted 1972, 1974, 1975, 1977, 1979, 1980

—

—

Made and printed in Great Britain
by Richard Clay (The Chaucer Press) Ltd,
Bungay, Suffolk
Set in Monotype Bembo

All applications to perform this play should be made to
A. P. Watt & Son,
26/28 Bedford Row,
London WC1R 4HL

# INTRODUCTION

WHEN Henrik Ibsen sent off the manuscript of *Brand* to his publisher in October 1865, he was already thirty-seven, and had endured two years of his self-imposed exile from Norway. In the fallow period that followed he began casting about for the inspiration to begin something new. 'I have work to do and energy enough to kill a bear,' he wrote in the following May; yet, in fact, he was to go through the whole of 1866 without writing a word of any new work. Years later he claimed that '*Peer Gynt* followed *Brand* almost of his own accord', but either he must have meant that the rapscallion Peer is the antithesis of the over-conscientious Brand, or else he had conveniently forgotten his struggles to find a new subject.

In Scandinavia in those days, Ibsen could reasonably have expected *Brand* to be in the bookshops by Christmas. In fact, it was not published till March 1866, and, though it quickly ran into four editions, it was some time before the royalties began to reach Ibsen in Rome. A letter that he wrote about this time to his friend Bjørnson ends:

P.S. I'm taking you at your word, my dear Bjørnson, and posting my letter to you without a stamp. I don't like doing it, but I have no choice.

In the same month he sent a petition to King Karl begging him to intercede with the Storthing (Parliament) to get him either the Poet's Stipend that they had refused him before he left Norway, or, failing that, a travel grant:

The first-fruits of my foreign travel have been my poem *Brand*. It has attracted attention abroad as well as at home, but I cannot live on expressions of gratitude. The royalties from my publisher, though most generous in the circumstances, are not enough to let me go on living abroad – nor indeed even enough to provide for my immediate needs.

Certainly when, at about this time, some less responsible members of the Scandinavian Club in Rome mischievously held a ballot to find the shabbiest of their number, Ibsen was voted easily the winner. As he had always been particularly sensitive about his appearance, and in his student days had preferred to go without meals rather than look poor, he must have been desperately hard up during these months, and now he had a wife and a young son to support.

At last the royalties from *Brand* began to come through, and Ibsen, with his first real success at last, was able to appear at the Club in a velvet jacket with a new shirt and gloves. By May he was writing to Hegel his publisher with the good news that the King's intervention had gained him a pension of 400 specie dollars (about £90). He went on:

> I shall soon be able to let you know what work I mean to start on. More than ever I feel that I want to get seriously to work on the *Emperor Julian* play that I have been considering for the past two years.

This was the play that eventually turned into the long and immensely tedious *Emperor and Galilean*. In August he wrote: 'I doubt if my new work will be finished by the autumn.' This was a reasonable doubt, since he hadn't even started on it. This letter, incidentally, enclosed a note to Edvard Grieg, who was the brother of Ibsen's friend Jon Grieg who had translated *The Pretenders* into German. Unfortunately the note has not been preserved, but it certainly had nothing to do with the famous incidental music.

Success changed Ibsen in several ways; it altered not only his dress and the cut of his beard, but also his whole outlook. Even his handwriting changed from something rather scratchy and immature to a clear well-formed script. The tone of his letters, which had been full of resentment against Norway and the Norwegians, changed miraculously. He was living, he wrote, 'very comfortably and cheaply' in Frascati, in a state 'of fairy-tale happiness'. In October he wrote to Hegel:

> If it's not too much trouble, would you advance me the money and get someone to buy me a lottery ticket . . . ? Not that I expect to win anything, but there's an excitement about it that appeals to me.

It is pleasant to find that later he did in fact win something in the Danish State Lottery.

The following month he tells Hegel that he is thinking of a work set in the period of King Christian IV. This must be the play about Magnus Heinesson that he had been making notes for before he left Norway, but which in fact he never finished. This letter goes on:

I'm turning over one or two other ideas in my mind . . . which only shows that none of them is really mature yet; I'm sure, though, that I shall be able to send you a finished MS. in the summer.

All that happened, though, was that he put both *Julian* and *Magnus Heinesson* aside again and worked on a revision of his early *Love's Comedy*, putting it into more colloquial speech. He was restless and irritable – especially after a drink or two. At last, early in January 1867, he wrote to Hegel again:

. . . and now I must tell you that my new work is progressing well and will be finished, barring accidents, by early summer. It will be a long dramatic poem, and its central figure will be one of those fantastic half-legendary characters from the Norwegian country tales of modern times. It will be nothing like *Brand*. I have started the first act, and the thing grows as I work at it. I'm sure you'll like it. But for the time being, please keep it a secret.

Incidentally, just as Peer Gynt himself would have done, Ibsen seems to have confused the inspiration with the actual words on paper; this letter is dated 5.1.67, but the date on the manuscript of the first draft shows that it was not started till a fortnight later.

Ibsen was something of an expert on Norwegian country legends; several times between 1857 and 1863, while the theatres where he was working were closed, he had been given a travel grant to go into the country and collect folk-songs and stories. Though most commentators give Asbjørnsen's *Norwegian Folk Tales* (Copenhagen, 1848) as Ibsen's source for the stories of Peer, we know that Ibsen (though he had certainly read Asbjørnsen) had travelled in the Gudbrandsdal, where he would have been almost certain to come across the Peer Gynt legends for himself.

Once he had started on the play, he wrote with a relaxed gaiety that was unusual for him. 'So far away from one's potential readers,' he wrote, 'one becomes reckless.' Soon he was feeling so pleased with what he had written that he sent a letter to the critic Clemens Petersen:

I have to thank you for more than your review of *Brand*. . . . I want to thank you for every word that you have written besides. I hope that you will find that in my new work I have taken an essential step forward.

He was soon to regret this letter bitterly.

By March he reported that the poem had 'progressed as far as the middle of the second act'. There would, he said, be five acts 'as far as I can judge at this stage', and he predicted that the complete work would 'run to about 250 pages'.

In the spring he left Rome for Ischia, where he worked so hard at the play that he seemed almost to lose himself in it. Vilhelm Bergsöe, who used to meet him in the evenings, reported that he was silent and remote, and that once he suddenly said:

'That's a fine field of hops down there.'

'Hops?' said Bergsöe, 'those are vines!'

'You're right, of course,' Ibsen admitted. 'Do you know, these days I'm continually having to pinch my arm to remind myself that I'm not back in Norway.' Like many other authors, Ibsen wrote best when he was working to a deadline, and he ended his letter to Hegel in March: 'If you wish, I shall be able to send you the MS. by July.' Presumably Hegel did not rise to the bait, for it is not until August that we find Ibsen writing:

Today I'm sending you, through the Consul General at Naples, the MS. of the first three acts of my new work, whose title is *Peer Gynt, a Dramatic Poem*. I hope the parcel will reach you at about the same time as this letter. . . . I expect to be able to send you the fourth act towards the end of this month, and the rest shortly afterwards.

All his working life, Ibsen was in this curious habit of sending the early acts of his plays to the publisher before the work was finished. Usually it was not quite so reckless as it seems, since he nearly always made at least one rough draft, and the final fair copy was the result of careful revision. With *Peer Gynt*, however, he seems to have stopped to make a fair copy of the first three acts before the last two acts were even planned; it was, as Ibsen admitted later, 'reckless and formless – written without any thought for the consequences'. By the end of Act One he had no very clear idea of what Peer would become, and even by the time he sent Act Four to Hegel, he had to ask him not to set up the list of characters, as he still was not sure what new people he might want to bring into the last act.

For once he felt free to introduce characters and settings according to the impulse of the moment. Bergsöe thinks that the whole desert episode was inspired by the savagely hot sirocco that swept Ischia in July 1867 (and in which Ibsen, unlike the other Northerners, thrived surprisingly well). He told Bergsöe at the time that, as each new section of the work presented itself, he felt 'like a horse straining to leap ahead'.

The covering letter to Hegel with the first three acts continued:

I shall be interested to hear what you think of the poem; I feel most hopeful about it. You might like to know that Peer Gynt was a real person. He lived in the Gudbrandsdal, probably at the end of the last century or the beginning of this. The peasants there still remember his name very well . . .

(which certainly reads as if Ibsen had first-hand knowledge of the legends):

. . . but nearly all that is known about him can be found in Asbjørnsen's *Norwegian Fairy Tales*. This means that I haven't much to build on, but that leaves me so much the freer. . . . And now I'm going to take advantage of your kind offer of some time ago, and ask you for an advance of 200 rix dollars. . . .

*Peer Gynt* was published in Copenhagen in November 1867. Ibsen wrote to Hegel:

You can be sure that today was a celebration for us. . . . I can't thank you enough for your splendidly generous offer of royalties. . . . If the critics are only favourable, I think the book will be widely read in Norway.

A day or two later, Ibsen heard from Bjørnson:

Dearest Ibsen,

So very many thanks for *Peer Gynt*; I don't remember ever having enjoyed a book so much before.

Ibsen had just started to answer this letter, when another post from Norway brought Petersen's review in *Fæderlandet*. It declared that *Peer Gynt* was 'not real poetry', that it was 'full of untenable ideas . . . and riddles so empty that there is no real answer to them'. It ended by calling the play 'a piece of polemical journalism'. Ibsen tore up his unfinished letter to Bjørnson and wrote another, in which his anger sometimes got the better of his syntax:

An hour ago I read Clemens Petersen's review. . . . If I were in Copenhagen, and someone there were as great a friend of mine as Clemens Petersen is of yours, I should have thrashed the life out of him before letting him commit such a deliberate crime against truth and justice. . . . You are quite at liberty to show him this letter. . . . You mustn't think that I'm a blind conceited fool; you can take my word that in my quieter moments I search and probe into my innermost parts – and just where it hurts most. . . . My book *is* poetry, and if it isn't now, it will be one day. . . .

Still, I'm glad of this injustice to me. . . . I feel that my anger is stimulating all my powers. If it is to be war, then war let it be! If I'm no poet, then I have nothing to lose; I shall try my luck as a photographer, and turn my attention to all my colleagues in the North, one after the other!

Certainly in his next play, *The League of Youth*, there were several portraits that hit home among his contemporaries in Norway, though none of them is recognizable as Petersen. Even Bjørnson thought that he recognized himself, and the split that this caused between the two old friends lasted for over ten years.

*Peer Gynt* was to be Ibsen's last play in verse. With *The League of Youth* he turned to photographically realistic plays in prose, and it was not long before he was proclaiming that 'verse is the enemy of Drama', and advising 'anyone who hopes to act, to be careful never to speak a word of verse'. It would be too much to suggest that this great step in Ibsen's development was directly due to Petersen's review, since Ibsen had already made and discarded some tentative efforts at prose plays, but as he was almost morbidly sensitive to unfavourable comments, this waspish criticism is sure to have left a scar.

Years later, at the end of his life, Ibsen wrote his strange and terrible play *When We Dead Wake*, where the guilt of the successful sculptor Rubek, at having made no more great statues but only 'mere portrait-busts', is symbolic of Ibsen's own self-reproach that he had turned to prose and eventually lost his talent for verse altogether. It is strangely prophetic that in *Peer Gynt* he should have made the Sighing in the Air reproach Peer:

> We are songs,
> you should have sung us.
>   A thousand times
> you have curbed and suppressed us.
> In the depths of your heart
> we have lain and waited. . . .
> We were never called forth –
>   now we poison your voice.

Petersen's was not the only unfavourable criticism of *Peer Gynt*. Georg Brandes wrote:

What great and noble powers have been wasted on this thankless stuff. Except in the fourth act – which has no connexion with what goes before or comes after – it is satire without wit, its irony is crude, and towards the end it becomes practically incomprehensible. Ibsen's poem is neither beautiful nor true; what acrid pleasure can any poet find in defiling humanity like this?

Perhaps both these critics had been expecting another *Brand* – something serious and uplifting – and were belabouring Ibsen, not for what he had actually written but because they themselves had been reading the book in the wrong key.

At any rate, the Norwegian and Danish public remembered

*Brand*; almost all the first edition was sold before publication, and there was a second edition of 2,000 within a fortnight. It was a long time, though, before *Peer Gynt* became as popular as *Brand*; by the turn of the century there had been only ten editions of *Peer Gynt* to fourteen of *Brand*. It is only in the present century that *Peer Gynt* has so far outstripped the earlier play that, particularly in the English-speaking world, *Brand* is comparatively unknown.

P. H. Wicksteed in his penetrating *Lectures on Henrik Ibsen* claims that:

In *Brand*, the hero is an embodied protest against the poverty of spirit and half-heartedness that Ibsen rebelled against in his countrymen; in *Peer Gynt* the hero is himself the embodiment of that spirit.

Though Brand may have been 'the Norwegian as he ought to be', if Peer is not exactly the Norwegian as he is, at any rate he is a gay caricature of the less estimable side of the author himself. In a speech in 1874 Ibsen admitted that:

Nobody can put a character on paper without – at any rate in part and at times – sitting as a model for it himself.

He was particularly conscious of his own failing of not being able to approach things directly. Once, as a young man, he was walking with a girl whom he had fallen in love with and had even proposed to, when he saw her father coming towards them; to his shame, and loss, he turned and ran rather than face him. Even in his writing he used to have the greatest difficulty in starting work each day – he would pace his study, stand gazing out of the window, or remember some chore that he could do for his wife. When he finally sat down he would find that his desk needed tidying, or he would simply sit and stare at the empty page. He used to devise all sorts of tricks, such as leaving a paragraph or even a sentence unfinished in the evening, so that he could start work more easily the next day. In the same way we find that Peer's great fault is that he always approaches things obliquely, and he willingly seizes on the Boyg's injunction to 'go round about', and in fact makes it practically his motto through life.

Like Peer, the young Ibsen was always going to do great things. The day after his first play *Catalina* was published (in an edition of 250 at the expense of his friend Ole Schulerud), the two boys moved to Christiania, where Ibsen was going to write two plays a year and make them both rich. Within a few months they were selling the 200 remaining copies to a grocer for wrapping paper so that they could buy food. 'And for a few days,' he wrote later, 'we wanted for nothing.'

Ibsen's own amorous adventures were certainly not as flamboyant as Peer's, but the episode of the Woman in Green and her ugly brat is a memory of the servant-girl, ten years older than himself, at the house of the chemist where he was apprenticed in Grimstad, and of her child for whom he had to pay maintenance for the next fourteen years.

Naturally there were several other models for Peer. According to Dr Brandes the immediate inspiration was 'a young Dane, a great boaster and spinner of yarns whom Ibsen used often to meet in Rome'. But Peer also contains a good deal of Ole Bull, the unbridled enthusiast who was manager of the Bergen Theatre when Ibsen worked there. Two other prominent Norwegians, the writer A. O. Vinje, and F. G. Lerche, a lawyer, each claimed that the other was the chief model. Lerche's main title to the doubtful honour was that he was said to make 'stating the facts' another term for downright lying; but Ibsen's old associates at home had no doubt that they recognized the witty and mercurial Vinje in Peer. However, in 1866 Vinje had attacked *Brand* as 'a joke too raving mad to be taken seriously', and unless Ibsen had suddenly become unusually forgiving, he is hardly likely to have immortalized his critic in such a lovable rapscallion as Peer. Moreover, Vinje was one of the champions of the movement for Language Reform that Ibsen hated so much, and that he satirized in Huhu's speeches in the Madhouse scene.

The other characters are little more than foils to Peer. Of Åse,

Ibsen wrote, 'My own mother, with some necessary exaggerations, was the model.' There is little to be said about Solveig, Ingrid, Anitra, and the rest; Shaw said that the enigmatic Button Moulder 'might be Brand's ghost'. The four travellers are merely caricatures of their various national types. A good deal has been written about the symbolism of the Boyg; two of the more reasonable guesses are that he represents 'the spirit of compromise', or that he is 'the ignorant and obstructive lethargy of the great mass of humanity'. Perhaps Ibsen was merely fascinated by the great formless Thing in the Gudbrandsdal legend, and saw how he could use it to underline Peer's particular weakness.

The Boyg is a troll, and trolls play a large part in the story. As they are an unfamiliar idea to most English readers, it might be as well to explain them. In Ibsen's day in the country districts of Norway, a belief in trolls was as near the surface as the belief in fairies and witches was in sixteenth-century England. But trolls have little in common with the pixies and brownies of English folk-lore; they are ugly and misshapen, and usually oafish and stupid and perhaps rather more akin to Milton's 'lubber fiend'. They may well be a folk-memory of some sub-human race like the Neanderthal Man, driven up into the mountains by the spread of *Homo sapiens*. They certainly have much more in common with the Abominable Snowman and the *fear liath mòr*, the Great Grey Man of the Cairngorms, than with Oberon and Titania. English fairies were seldom grotesque, and before Shakespeare romanticized them into tiny creatures who could creep into acorn-cups, they were almost the same size as ourselves – for there are many legends of fairies marrying mortals. Even Shakespeare fell into some double-thinking, for Oberon had loved the Amazonian Hippolyta, and Titania could lie on her flowery bank with Bottom. But in reading *Peer Gynt* we must clear all this cobweb stuff from our minds and think of the trolls only as grotesque and malevolent. They have a lot in common with the *id* of the Freudians – an embodiment of the primitive urges of mankind. If any stage producer feels tempted to use children to play his trolls, he should be careful to choose only very ugly children.

In England, ironically enough, *Peer Gynt* is much better known from Grieg's incidental music than from Ibsen's text. Ibsen had never meant *Peer Gynt* for the stage, any more than Hardy meant *The Dynasts* or Browning *Pippa*; it was merely that after his long apprenticeship in the theatre he wrote most easily in dialogue, and the dramatic form was a popular and fashionable one for long narrative poems. It was not until 1874, seven years after its publication, that Ibsen wrote to Edvard Grieg:

> I am writing to ask if you would cooperate with me in a certain project: I am thinking of arranging *Peer Gynt* for the stage; would you compose the music?
>
> The first act I shall keep in full, with only a few cuts. . . . Peer Gynt's monologue on pp. 23–5 I want treated either as a *melodrame* or recitative. The wedding scene must be made, by means of a ballet, into something more than it is in the book, and a special dance will have to be composed which must continue softly to the end of the act.
>
> In Act Two, the music for the scene with the herd-girls must be left to the composer, though it must have some devilry in it. . . .

He then goes on to set out in great detail the music that he wants for the rest of Acts Two and Three. For a man with his practical experience in the theatre and his fine sense of the dramatic, he had some very strange ideas about Act Four – the act that Dr Brandes thought the only worth-while part of the whole play:

> Almost the whole of Act Four could be cut. Instead, I think there should be a great musical tone-picture to suggest Peer Gynt's travels all over the world – American, English and French airs might be brought in. . . . The chorus of Anitra and the girls should be heard from behind the curtain with an orchestral accompaniment. During this music the curtain should rise to show a distant dream-picture of . . . Solveig, now middle-aged, in the sun outside her hut. After her song the curtain would fall slowly, with the music continuing but changing to a suggestion of the storm at sea that opens Act Five. . . . These are my ideas; will you let me know if you are willing to undertake the work? . . . I mean to ask 400 specie dollars for it, to be divided equally between us. I feel sure that we can count on the play also being produced in Stockholm and Copenhagen.

Ibsen must have felt sure that Grieg would agree, or he would hardly have gone into quite so much detail. Grieg, however, had many doubts about undertaking a project with so many difficulties – not the least of which was clearly going to be the author himself. Among other things it meant shelving his opera *Olav Trygvesson*, which, in fact, he never finished. In the end he somehow managed to convince himself that it was 'only a question of some fragments here and there', and he agreed to tackle it. Four months later he was complaining that:

*Peer Gynt* is the most unmusical of all subjects. It hangs over me like a nightmare, and I doubt if I shall finish it before the spring.

In fact, it was the following September before he completed the score. Fortunately Herr Josephson, the Manager of the Christiania Theatre, would not agree with the massive disembowelling of the text that Ibsen had proposed. He suggested instead a great number of discreet small cuts that left practically no scars, and even Ibsen admitted that this was a great improvement.

*Peer Gynt*, with Grieg's incidental music, was first performed in February 1876. Though Ibsen was not altogether satisfied with the music, he admitted that it 'sugared the pill so that the public could swallow it'. To our ears today it seems even to over-sugar it, though perhaps we have become too familiar with the two Suites (which Grieg prepared later) tinkled out in tea-shops. Possibly Grieg, of whom it has been said that 'his music casts no shadow', was the wrong person to set an astringent play like *Peer Gynt*. Certainly much of the music sounds almost ridiculously inappropriate today; for example, the piece that we know as 'Morning' (literally 'Morning Mood'), which in the Palm Court conjures up at once a picture of the early sun lighting the snowy slopes in the crisp Norwegian air, is meant to accompany Peer's disillusioned awakening in the hot Sahara when he finds himself stripped of all he had. To Grieg, and probably to its hearers in 1876, it must have seemed more acid. Of the music that was to accompany the dance of the pig-faced troll princess in the Dovrë hall, where 'the cows give cakes, and the oxen ale', Grieg wrote:

For the Hall of the Mountain King I have written something that so reeks of cowpats, ultra-Norwegianism, and 'to-thyself-be-enough-ness' that I literally can't bear to hear it, though I hope that the irony will make itself felt.

Yet to us this music is more likely to call up a picture of a kindergarten dancing-class.

A stage producer today is bound to find that the music holds up the action unbearably, but we cannot blame Grieg for this; it was designed to cover the long waits that the setting of realistic scenery imposed on theatres not equipped with modern machinery. Be that as it may, the name of Peer Gynt is so linked with Grieg's music in the public mind that anyone who tried to stage the play without at least some of the too-familiar melodies would be sure of a disappointed audience.

Archer, writing in 1907, said that *Peer Gynt* had never been played on the English stage. Luckily there have been several outstanding productions since Archer's day. In 1923 Robert Atkins produced it at the Old Vic with Russell Thorndike as Peer; eleven years later Tyrone Guthrie produced Ralph Richardson in the part at the New Theatre; and there was a BBC Television production by Royston Morley in 1954, with Peter Ustinov. As far as I know there has never been a professional production of the full text, but in the late twenties an adventurous amateur society near Woolwich gave a really excellent performance of the play in its entirety.

\*

Unfortunately it is almost inevitable that a translation must fall short of the original, and with a poem the diminution is particularly glaring. *Peer Gynt* in its original Norwegian is in rhymed verse. It is gay, galloping verse, with rhymes that are often double or triple, and as ingenious and outrageous as any that Robert Browning or W. S. Gilbert ever devised. The lines are mostly in couplets but sometimes in quatrains. The metre is based on four stresses to a line, but with a varying number of syllables to the foot;

iambuses, trochees, spondees, dactyls, and anapaests come tumbling over each other to give the poem a splendid vitality.

When Archer wanted to put the play into English, Ibsen wrote that he would rather have it left untranslated than rendered into prose. Certainly to rob the work of its varied metres would be to take most of the fun out of it; on the other hand, it would be impossible to combine Ibsen's complicated and witty rhyming with an even moderately accurate translation. I have therefore followed Archer in using unrhymed verse, keeping to Ibsen's four-stressed line, though I have not always slavishly followed his exact scansion at the expense of the meaning in English. Indeed, to compensate for the loss of Ibsen's adventurous rhymes (and remembering A. E. Housman's dictum that in English while 'blank verse can be written in lines of ten or six syllables, a series of octosyllables ceases to be verse if they are not rhymed') I have deliberately tended to vary the metre a little more than Ibsen does, in case the lines should settle down into monotony. I have been especially free with Ibsen's metre where he writes in quatrains of alternate lines of eight and seven syllables – a form that in English is hard to bear without rhyme.

Ibsen's language, especially in the first three acts, is simple and even rustic. I have not tried to reproduce this by using English dialect, as I feel that it might set the play too firmly in the soft green fields of some specific English county. Instead, I have aimed at a simple colloquial speech. English is peculiar in that we tend in ordinary speech to use accusative pronouns after the verb 'to be'. Though there is no warrant for it in the original, I have followed our slipshod colloquial practice, rather than make the country people sound pedantic and unconvincing by saying 'It is I'.

In Ibsen's letters to his publisher he stressed his desire that the lines should start with a small letter except where there would normally be a capital in prose. In spite of the danger that this might give a slightly precious effect, I have obeyed Ibsen's wish.

P.W.

# PEER GYNT

# The Characters

Åse, *a farmer's widow*
Peer Gynt, *her son*
Two Old Women, *with sacks of corn*

Aslak, *a smith*
Wedding Guests, a Master of Ceremonies, Musicians, *etc.*
A Pair of Settlers
Solveig and little Helga, *their daughters*
The Farmer at Hægstad
Ingrid, *his daughter*
The Bridegroom and his Parents

Three Upland Herd-Girls
A Woman in Green
The Old Man of the Dovrë
A Troll Courtier; many other Trolls; Troll Youths and Girls; a few
    Witches; Old Dwarfs; Hobgoblins; Gnomes, *etc.*

An Ugly Boy
A Voice in the Dark
Birds' Cries
Kari, *a cottager's wife*

Mr Cotton; Monsieur Ballon; Herr von Eberkopf; Herr Trum-
    peterstråle, *travellers*
A Thief and a Receiver
Anitra, *daughter of a Bedouin Chief*
Arabs; Slaves; Dancing Girls, *etc.*

The Statue of Memnon, *a singing part*; the Sphinx at Gizeh, *a mute*
Professor Begriffenfeldt, Ph.D., *Director of the Lunatic Asylum at
    Cairo*
Huhu, *a language reformer from the Malabar Coast*; Hussein, *an Eastern
    Minister of State*; a Fellah *carrying a Royal Mummy*
Several Inmates of the Asylum; their Keepers

A Norwegian Skipper and his Crew
A Strange Passenger

A Priest; a Funeral Party; a Bailiff
A Button Moulder
A Thin Person

The action, which begins in the early years of the century and ends about our own day,[1] takes place partly in the Gudbrandsdal and on the surrounding mountains, and partly on the Coast of Morocco, in the Sahara Desert, in a Lunatic Asylum in Cairo, at sea, etc.

1. Ibsen was writing in 1867.
The Gudbrandsdal (pronounced *Good*-bran's-dahl) is a long valley in the Opland province, that is to say in the south-western heel of Norway, to the north of Oslo and the north-east of Bergen.

# ACT ONE

*A wooded slope near Åse's farm, with a stream flowing by, beyond which is an old mill. It is a hot summer's day.* PEER GYNT, *a sturdy youth of twenty, comes down the path;* ÅSE *his mother, who is short and slight, follows him, scolding angrily.*

ÅSE:[1] That's a lie, Peer!

PEER GYNT [*without stopping*]: No it isn't!

ÅSE: Well then, swear to it! Swear it's true!

PEER GYNT: Swear? Why should I?

ÅSE:                         Pah! You dare not!
   Lies and nonsense, all of it!

PEER GYNT [*stopping*]: Every blessed word of it's true!

ÅSE [*standing in front of him*]: Shame! How dare you face
      your mother?
   First, just when the work is hardest,
   off you run for months together
   hunting reindeer in the snow;
   next you come home with your gun lost,
   no food, and your coat in ribbons;
   now, to crown it all, you're trying
   shamelessly to take me in
   with a pack of huntsman's lies! . . .
   Well, where did you find this buck?

PEER GYNT: West of Gjendin.[2]

1. Pronounced *Aw*-seh. To be tiresomely pedantic, *Peer Gynt* should be pronounced Pair Günt.

2. In Ibsen's day it was spelt thus; the modern spelling is *Gendin*, but I have kept the form that Ibsen used, to remind readers of the pronunciation, which is *Yen*-deen. Gjendin Ridge is a sharp knife-edge between Lake

ÅSE [*with a scornful laugh*]:     Very likely!

PEER GYNT: While I sheltered from the weather,
hidden by a clump of bushes,
he was scraping at the snow-crust
after moss –

ÅSE [*as before*]: A likely story!

PEER GYNT: I stood listening, hardly breathing,
– heard the scraping of his hoof-tip –
till I saw one branching antler;
so I carefully crept forward
on my belly through the stones,
till around a boulder's cover
I could peep. . . . You never saw
such a buck! So sleek and fat!

ÅSE: Goodness gracious!

PEER GYNT:                Then I fired!
Down the buck crashed on the hillside,
but the instant that he stumbled
I was straddled on his shoulders
with his left ear in my grasp,
just about to plunge my knife in
where the backbone joins the skull.
Hey! The ugly creature bellowed –
leaping to his feet at once!
As he rose, the sudden lurching
jerked my sheath-knife out of my hand;
but his antlers held my legs pinned,
tightly gripped against his loins,
holding me as in a vice.

---

Bygdin and Lake Gjendin in the Jotunheim. The local boast is that if a man stands on the ridge with outstretched arms and drops a stone from each hand, they will roll straight into the water on either side.

Then, with a sudden leap, he bounded
right along the ridge of Gjendin!

ÅSE [*involuntarily*]: Heaven preserve us!

PEER GYNT: Have you ever
seen that mountain ridge at Gjendin?
All of half a mile it stretches,
sheer and sharp as the blade of a scythe.
Either side, if you look downwards,
over glacier, scar, and hillside,
you can see, across the ash-grey
scree, deep into brooding waters
dark as if asleep – and more than
thirteen hundred yards below![1]

All the ridge's length, we two
cut our way against the wind.
Such a colt I never rode!

There in mid-air straight before us
seemed to hang the blazing sun.
Halfway down towards the waters
tawny backs of eagles hovered
through the wide and dizzy void,
till they swung like specks behind us.

On the shores below, the ice-floes
crashed and splintered, yet no murmur
reached us, only swirling mist-shapes
leapt like dancers, weaving – singing –
round about our eyes and ears.

ÅSE [*swaying*]: Oh, God help me!

---

1. Peer Gynt is exaggerating again. According to Asbjørnsen's informant, the ridge is 'not nearly as high as the Rondë hills, but it's over seven hundred ells high'. The English ell is rather more than a yard, but the Norwegian (more accurately, since the word is derived from *ulna* – the forearm) is rather less. 'Yard' seems a reasonable compromise.

PEER GYNT:                         Suddenly
up a cock-grouse rocketed
from the rocks where he'd been crouching –
flapping, cackling, terrified –
right beneath the buck's foot, balanced
sheer above a break-neck cliff.

    With a start as high as heaven,
turning half about, the reindeer
plunged us both down to the depths!

        [ÅSE *reels, reaching for the trunk of a tree.* PEER
        GYNT *continues*]

At our backs, the gloomy rock-face –
under us, the deep abyss!

    First we hurtled through a cloud-sheet,
next we split a flock of sea-gulls
scattering them in all directions
while they filled the air with screeching.

    Downwards without pause we hurtled;
till below us something glistened
whitish, like a reindeer's belly. . . .
Mother, it was our reflection
shooting from the glassy water
with the self-same crazy motion
as ours, rushing down to meet it.

ÅSE [*gasping for breath*]: Peer! For God's sake tell me
    quickly!

PEER GYNT: Buck from the air and buck from the surface
clashed their horns in a single moment,
so that the foam splashed all about us.

    There we were, then, in the water!
He swam, I hung on behind him,
till at long, long last we struggled
somehow to the northern shore. . . .

I came home –

ÅSE:         Yes, but the buck, Peer?

PEER GYNT: Oh, he's probably still there!

      [*Snapping his fingers, he turns on his heels and adds*]

If you find him, you can have him!

ÅSE: And you didn't break your neck there –

smash a leg, or rick your spine?

Praise and thanks to God Almighty

for the way he saved my boy!

True, you've gone and torn your breeches . . .

still, that's hardly worth a mention

when I think what a disaster

such a leap as that could mean. . . .

      [*Suddenly she stops, looking at him wide-eyed and*
      *open-mouthed; for a long time she is speechless, then*
      *at last she breaks out*]

Oh, you spin yarns like the devil!

God above, how you can lie!

All this nonsense you've come out with,

I remember now – I heard it

when I was a lass of twenty!

That's the tale of Gudbrand Glesnë,[1]

not of *you* –

PEER GYNT: Of both of us;

such things happen more than once!

ÅSE [*angrily*]: Yes, a lie can be refurbished,

---

1. Like Peer Gynt, Glesnë was a real person. He, too, appears in Asbjørn-sen's *Folk Tales*. Asbjørnsen's friend tells him: 'He was a clever hunter from the Western Hills; he was married to the grandmother of the lad you met yesterday.'

Ibsen makes Peer live up to his reputation in real life – of always claiming other men's adventures as his own.

The letter ë does not exist in Norwegian; I have followed Archer in using it, here and elsewhere, to remind the reader that the final *e* must be sounded.

tricked out fresh with boasts and bragging,
dressed up in a brand new skin
to disguise its scrawny carcass –
and that's just what you've been doing,
titivating it so finely
with your talk of eagle's backs
 - not to mention other nonsense –
every single word a lie!
Such a tale of breathless danger
that I don't know, now you've finished,
what I've heard and what I haven't!

PEER GYNT: If a *man* had talked like that
I'd beat the daylight out of him!

ÅSE [*weeping*]: Would to heaven I was sleeping
peacefully below the ground!
Tears and prayers mean nothing to you!
You're a wastrel – now and always!

PEER GYNT: Dearest pretty little mother,
every word you've said is true,
so cheer up, now –

ÅSE:               Hold your tongue!
How d'you think I can be cheerful
when my son's a pig like you?
Haven't I, a helpless widow,
every reason to be bitter
since I'm always put to shame?
     [*She weeps again.*]
Just how much have we got left now
from your grandad's palmy days?
Where are all the sacks of money
left us by old Rasmus Gynt?
Yes, your father set wings to 'em,
emptying them just like sand –

buying land in all directions –
riding in a gilded coach. . . .
Where's the money that he wasted
on his great mid-winter feasts,
when each guest sent glass and bottle
smashing on the wall behind him?

PEER GYNT: What's become of last year's snow?[1]

ÅSE: Hold your tongue when your mother's talking!
Look at the farmhouse! Half the windows
broken – stuffed with dirty rags!
Fences broken down, the cowhouse
empty – open to the weather;
fields and meadows lying fallow;
every month the bailiffs in!

PEER GYNT: That's enough of pretty speeches!
Often when our luck seemed lowest
things turned out as good as ever!

ÅSE: Salt's been sprinkled where our luck grew.
Goodness, you're a fine one, you are!
Just as pert and cocky still –
jaunty as the day the parson,
coming here from Copenhagen,
asked you what your Christian name was –
saying princes, where he came from,
couldn't boast the talents you had;
till, in gratitude, your father
pressed a horse and carriage on him
just because he praised you nicely!
Huh! How good things were in those days!
Parsons, officers, and such-like

---

1. Villon's famous line is well known in Norway, but to translate this phrase as 'the snows of yesteryear' would suggest a literacy that would be quite wrong for Peer at this stage.

dropped in every day at mealtimes –
gorged themselves to bursting-point!
Yes, it's not till things go badly
that you find out who your friends are;
since the day when 'Jon o' the Moneybags'[1]
took to the road with a pedlar's pack,
we've been quiet here – no more callers. ....

[*She wipes her eyes with her apron.*]

You're a great big strapping fellow,
you should be a prop and buttress –
helping out your poor old mother –
farming hard to get our living,
fostering the bit that's left us.

[*She weeps again.*]

Goodness knows it's precious little
help I've had from you, you lout!
When you're home, you're by the fireside
poking at the coals and embers;
and in town you scare the girls you
meet at the Assembly Room –
get in fights with gutter-snipes –
shaming me at every turn!

PEER GYNT [*moving away*]: Let me be!

ÅSE [*following him*]:         And don't you tell me
that it wasn't you who started
that big dust-up down at Lundë
where you fought like any dog!
Wasn't it you who fought the blacksmith
Aslak?[2] Yes, you broke his arm ...
well, at the very least you twisted
one of his fingers out of joint!

PEER GYNT: Who's been telling you all that nonsense?

1. Literally 'Jon with the bushel'.      2. Pronounced *Uss*-luk.

ÅSE [*angrily*]: The cottagers' wives could hear the yells!
PEER GYNT [*rubbing his elbow*]: Yes. But it was I who
    yelled!
ÅSE: You?
PEER GYNT: Yes mother – I got beaten.
ÅSE: What d'you mean?
PEER GYNT:          He's very strong.
ÅSE: Who is?
PEER GYNT: Aslak. Don't I know it?
ÅSE: Shame on you – shame! Oh, I could spit!
  Letting such a lazy drunkard,
  such a brawler, such a tosspot,
  such a good-for-nothing, beat you!
     [*Weeping again*]
  Haven't I enough to plague me
  without suffering this shame?
  Really this is going *too* far!
  Even though he may be strong,
  what's in that to make you weak?
PEER GYNT: If I beat, or if I'm beaten –
  either way you start your howling!
     [*He laughs.*]
  Cheer up, mother –
ÅSE:            Why? Was that
  another lie?
PEER GYNT: It was – for once!
  So you might as well stop crying.
     [*He clenches his left fist.*]
  Look! *This* was the tongs I used
  when I bent the blacksmith double,
  and my right fist was my hammer.
ÅSE: Oh you brawler! Soon you'll have me
  in my grave, the way you're going!

PEER GYNT: Shall I? You're worth something better –
twenty thousand times as good!
Darling ugly little mother,
just you take my word for it
all the town shall do you honour.
Only wait till I've done something –
something really marvellous!

ÅSE [*with a snort*]: You!

PEER GYNT:                    Who knows what I might do?

ÅSE: Yes – if just for once you had the
wit to patch your breeches' seat!

PEER GYNT [*hotly*]: I'll become a king – an emperor!

ÅSE: Oh, God help me – now he's losing
any little sense he had!

PEER GYNT: I shall do it! Give me time!

ÅSE: 'Give you time, you'll become a Prince!'
So the saying goes, I think.

PEER GYNT: You'll see, mother.

ÅSE:                    Hold your tongue!
You're as mad as mad can be!
   Well – perhaps it's *possible*
something might be made of you
if you didn't waste your time in
spinning lies and such-like nonsense.
That girl down at Hægstad[1] liked you –
you'd have won a handsome dowry
if you'd really wanted to.

PEER GYNT: Do you think so?

ÅSE:                    Why, the old man's
far too weak to thwart his daughter.
Oh, I know he can be stubborn;
Ingrid always gets her way, though;

1. Pronounced *Hegg*-stuh.

32

where she leads, the dotard follows
grumbling, step by step behind her.
    [*She starts crying again.*]
Oh Peer, only think of it!
She has money – expectations;
if you only had a mind to,
you'd be wearing bridegroom's garments
not these dirty rags and tatters.

PEER GYNT [*quickly*]: Very well, we'll go and ask her!

ÅSE: Where?

PEER GYNT: At Hægstad.

ÅSE:                 You're unlucky!
That way's barred to you, you'll find.

PEER GYNT: Why is that?

ÅSE:                   Well, to my sorrow,
you're too late – you've missed your moment.

PEER GYNT: Oh?

ÅSE [*sobbing*]:     While you were riding reindeer
high above the Western mountains,
she was promised to Mads Moen.[1]

PEER GYNT: What? The man the girls all laugh at?

ÅSE: Yes, she's going to marry him.

PEER GYNT: You wait here – I'll go and harness
up the horse and cart.
    [*He starts to go.*]

ÅSE:              The wedding
is tomorrow. Save your pains.

PEER GYNT: Pooh! I'm going there this evening!

---

1. The name of a Sheriff in the West in the 1840s. Ibsen's biographer Halvdan Koht suggests that this man may have been responsible for enforcing against Ibsen the maintenance order on his son by the servant-girl at the apothecary's at Grimstad. Mads is a diminutive of Matthew; the name is pronounced Muds *Moh*-en.

ÅSE: We're a laughing stock already,
　do you want to make things worse?
PEER GYNT: Cheer up! It'll be all right.
　　　　[*Laughing and shouting at the same time*]
　Hey! We'll do without the cart –
　there's no time to catch the mare!
　　　　[*He picks her up.*]
ÅSE: Put me down!
PEER GYNT:　　　　I'm carrying you
　over to the wedding-feast!
　　　　[*He wades out into the stream.*]
ÅSE: Help! God save us! Peer, we'll drown!
PEER GYNT: I was born for something higher!
ÅSE: True! You'll end up on a gallows!
　　　　[*Pulling his hair*]
　Oh, you beast!
PEER GYNT:　　　　Keep very still now –
　here the bottom's slippery!
ÅSE: Fool!
PEER GYNT: Yes, simply use your tongue –
　that does no one any damage!
　Ah, it's getting shallower. . . .
ÅSE: Don't let go of me!
PEER GYNT:　　　　　　Hi! Hup!
　Now we'll play at Peer and reindeer –
　　　　[*Prancing about*]
　I'm the reindeer, you be Peer!
ÅSE: Oh, I don't know *who* I am!
PEER GYNT: There! we're back on dry ground now.
　　　　[*Wading ashore*]
　Now! Just give your steed a kiss
　as a payment for his trouble.
ÅSE [*boxing his ears*]: Here's my thanks for all the trouble!

PEER GYNT: Ow! You paid that in hard cash!

ÅSE: Put me down!

PEER GYNT:          Yes – at the wedding!
  Be my spokesman – you're so clever,
  you can talk to that old dotard . . .
  say Mads Moen is a milksop –

ÅSE: Down!

PEER GYNT: And when you've done that, tell him
  just the sort of lad Peer Gynt is!

ÅSE: Take my word for it, I mean to!
  Such a character I'll give you –
  top to toe, a perfect likeness;
  yes, I'll tell him, fair and square,
  all the devil's tricks you play –

PEER GYNT: Oh?

ÅSE [*kicking out in anger*]: And I won't end my story
  till the old man calls his dogs out
  just as if you were a tramp.

PEER GYNT: Hm, I think I'll go without you.

ÅSE: I shall follow, all the same!

PEER GYNT: You're not strong enough, dear mother!

ÅSE: Aren't I though? Why, I'm so angry
  I could crush those rocks to powder –
  I could crack flints in my teeth!
  Put me down!

PEER GYNT:          Yes, if you'll promise –

ÅSE: No, I mean to go there with you,
  just to tell them what you're like!

PEER GYNT: No you won't; you're staying here.

ÅSE: Never! I'll be at the party.

PEER GYNT: I won't let you.

ÅSE:                    You can't stop me!

PEER GYNT: On the mill-roof – that's where *you*'ll go!

[*He lifts her up there;* ÅSE *screams.*]

ÅSE: Lift me down!

PEER GYNT:          Well, will you listen –?

ÅSE: Fiddlesticks!

PEER GYNT:          Dear mother – please!

ÅSE [*throwing a clod of turf at him*[1]]:
          Lift me down this instant, Peer!

PEER GYNT: Gladly – if I only dared!
                    [*Coming nearer*]
          Now remember – sit there quietly;
          don't start lashing out and kicking,
          loosening the anchor-stones,
          otherwise you'll hurt yourself.
          You might fall –

ÅSE:                    You monster, you!

PEER GYNT: Gently now!

ÅSE:                              You should have been
          blown away like any changeling.[2]

PEER GYNT: Fie now, Mother!

ÅSE:                              Pooh!

PEER GYNT:                              You ought to
          give your blessing on my venture.
          Will you? . . . Well?

ÅSE:                    I ought to thrash you
          hard – great lumpkin that you are.

PEER GYNT: Well, good-bye then, dearest mother.
          Wait there – I won't keep you long.

---

1. This might seem unlikely from the top of the roof, but the thatch has become overgrown with grass. The stones, a few lines later, are the boulders that hold down the thatch against the gales.

2. The traditional way of getting rid of a changeling (a puny baby substituted for the rightful child by the trolls) was to let it be blown up the chimney by spells.

[*He starts to go, but turns to lift a warning finger.*]
Don't forget, you're not to struggle!
[*He goes.*]

ÅSE: Peer! . . . God help me, now he's going!
Reindeer-rider! Liar! Hi!
Listen, will you? . . . No, he's gone
across the fields. [*Shouting*] Help! Help, I'm giddy!
[*Two OLD WOMEN with sacks on their backs come
down towards the mill.*]

FIRST WOMAN: Bless us, who's that shouting?

ÅSE:                                        Me!

SECOND WOMAN: Åse! You've gone up in life!

ÅSE: What good's that to me? God help me,
I shall soon go up to heaven!

FIRST WOMAN: Pleasant journey!

ÅSE:                              Fetch a ladder,
get me down. That devil Peer –

SECOND WOMAN: You mean your son?

ÅSE:                                  Now you can say
you've *seen* the way he carries on.

FIRST WOMAN: We'll bear witness.

ÅSE:                              Only help me,
I must get to Hægstad quickly.

SECOND WOMAN: Is he there?

FIRST WOMAN:                  You'll be revenged, then –
Aslak's going to the feast!

ÅSE [*wringing her hands*]: Oh, may God preserve my boy!
They'll have his life before they've done!

FIRST WOMAN: Yes, we've heard reports about them,
take my word, that's what they'll do!

SECOND WOMAN: Now she's gone completely crazy!
[*Calling up the hill*]
Eyvind! Anders! Hi, come here!

A MAN'S VOICE:
  What's wrong?
SECOND WOMAN: Peer Gynt has perched his mother
  right up on the mill-house roof![1]

*

*A little hill covered with bushes and heather. The road, which
runs at the back, is shut off by a fence.* PEER GYNT *comes along
a footpath; he goes quickly to the fence and stands looking out at
the view that is spread before him.*

PEER GYNT: That's Hægstad farm. I'll soon be down
    there.
        [*He starts to climb the fence, then stops to think.*]
  I wonder if Ingrid's[2] indoors by herself.
        [*He shades his eyes and peers into the distance.*]
  No, people with presents are swarming like midges....
  Hm, I'd do better to go home again.
        [*He brings his leg back over the fence.*]
  They always whisper behind your back
  and their sniggering seems to burn right through you.[3]
        [*He goes a step or two away from the fence, and plucks
        idly at a bush.*]
  If only I'd had a drink or two –
  or if I could get there without people seeing –
  or if no one knew me.... A really strong drink
  would be best, then their laughter wouldn't matter.

1. Ibsen made no division of this play into numbered scenes. As with
Shakespeare, those that appear in modern editions have been added by later
editors. The metre changes from scene to scene (and sometimes even in
mid-scene), while still keeping to the four-stressed line.
2. Strictly speaking should be pronounced *Een*-gri.
3. Ibsen himself was morbidly sensitive to ridicule.

[*He suddenly turns round, as if startled, and then hides among the bushes. A few people with gifts of food pass by on their way to the wedding-feast.*]

A MAN [*in conversation*]: His father drank, and his mother is sickly. . . .

A WOMAN: Small wonder the boy has turned out such a dunce.

[*They pass on. After a little,* PEER GYNT *comes out, blushing with shame. He peers after them.*]

PEER GYNT [*under his breath*]: Could it be me they were talking about?

[*With an exaggerated shrug*]

Oh well, let them gossip – it doesn't hurt *me*!

[*He throws himself on a bank of heather, and lies for a long time on his back with his hands behind his head, staring into the sky.*]

That's a funny shaped cloud – why it's just like a horse!
There's a man on its back – and a saddle – and bridle.
Behind it there rides an old witch on her broomstick –

[*Laughing quietly to himself*]

it's mother! She's shouting and screaming 'You beast!
Hi there! Peer!'

[*Gradually closing his eyes*]

Aha, now she's frightened!

Peer Gynt rides ahead with a whole host behind him,
    four gold shoes on his horse, silver crests on his harness.
And he's carrying gauntlets and sabre and scabbard.
    His surcoat is long, with a rich silken lining.
Fine are the henchmen who tread in his footsteps,
    but never a one sits so well on his charger,
and none of them sparkles like him in the sun.

    All down the highway the people are crowding,
raising their bonnets and staring aloft;

womenfolk curtsey, for everyone knows that
it's Emperor Peer with his thousand retainers.
  Glittering marks, and great twelve-shilling pieces
bounce in the roadway like pebbles around him;
  each of the townsmen grows rich as a baron. . . .
Then Peer Gynt in his glory sails over the ocean;
Engelland's[1] Prince stands and waits on the seashore,
and Engelland's maidens all follow his lead,
  Engelland's Emperor, Engelland's nobles
rise from their thrones as Peer Gynt gallops forward,
  and, doffing his crown, their Emperor says –

ASLAK THE SMITH [*to several others as they pass by beyond the fence*]:
  Why, look – there's that drunken swine, Peer Gynt!

PEER GYNT [*half rising*]: Why . . . Emperor –!

ASLAK [*leaning on the fence and grinning*]: Up on your feet
  with you, lad!

PEER GYNT: What the devil –? The blacksmith! Well,
  what do you want?

ASLAK [*to the others*]: He hasn't forgotten our scrimmage at
  Lundë!

PEER GYNT [*jumping up*]:
  Now just you clear off!

ASLAK:                         Oh, I certainly will!
  But where, my good man, have you been to since then?
  It was six weeks ago. Were you captured by trolls?

PEER GYNT: Ah, smith, I've had splendid adventures since
  then!

ASLAK [*winking at the others*]:
  Tell us them, Peer.

  1. This is Ibsen's spelling; the normal spelling of the word in Norwegian
is the same as our own. Engelland bears the same relation to England as the
Norroway of our Border Ballads does to Norway.

PEER GYNT: They'd be over your heads!

ASLAK [*after a moment*]:
Are you going to Hægstad?

PEER GYNT: No.

ASLAK: Not long ago
they were saying that *you* were the one the girl fancied!

PEER GYNT: You black crow –!

ASLAK [*backing a little*]: Now then, Peer, better
not lose your temper!
If Ingrid won't have you, there's plenty of others;
you're Jon Gynt's son, aren't you? Come down to the
feast,
there'll be maidens like lambkins, and middle-aged
widows –

PEER GYNT: Go to hell!

ASLAK: You'll be sure to find *someone*
who'll have you!
Good night, then; I'll give your respects to the bride.
[*They go, whispering and laughing.*]

PEER GYNT [*looking after them for a moment, then half turning
back with a shrug*]:
That Hægstad girl can choose whom she likes
for all I care. It won't worry me.
[*Looking down at himself*]
My trousers all tattered – dirty and torn –
if only I had something new to put on!
[*He stamps on the hillside.*]
I wish that I'd had a butcher's training,
I'd cut the sneering out of their throats!
[*Suddenly looking round*]
Who's that? Was there somebody laughing behind me?
I was certain I heard . . . . No, there's nobody there.
I'll go home to mother.

[*He starts to go up, but pauses to listen in the direction of the wedding party.*]

　　　　　　They're playing a dance!

[*He listens, staring, as he moves nearer step by step. His eyes shine, and he rubs his hands down his thighs.*]

What a swarm of young girls – eight or nine to a man!
Oh, death and damnation, I *must* join the party!
But what about mother, up there on the mill-house?

[*His eyes wander downwards again; he leaps up and down, laughing.*]

Hiya! Look how they're dancing the Halling![1]
Ah listen, that Guttorm's first-rate on the fiddle –
it ripples and sings like a stream at a waterfall.
And then all those girls – how they sparkle and glitter. . . .
Yes, hell and damnation, I *must* join the party!

[*With a bound, he leaps the fence and is off down the road.*]

\*

*The Courtyard at Hægstad, with the farm buildings at the back. There are many guests, and a lively dance is in progress in the courtyard. The fiddler is sitting at a table; the* MASTER OF CEREMONIES[2] *is standing in the doorway. Kitchen-maids pass backwards and forwards between the buildings. The older folk sit about gossiping.*

A WOMAN [*joining a group who are sitting on some logs*]:
The bride? Yes, of course she's crying a little,
but who'd pay any attention to that?

　　1. An energetic peasant dance in which the men try to kick the rafters.
　　2. Literally Master-Cook.

THE MASTER OF CEREMONIES [*in another group*]:
Come along now, good people, and empty the jar!

A MAN: Thank you, I will – but you fill up so quickly!

A BOY [*to the fiddler, as he runs past hand-in-hand with a girl*]:
Keep it up, Guttorm, and don't spare the cat-gut!

THE GIRL: Scrape till it rings out right over the meadows!

GIRLS [*in a ring round a boy who is dancing*]: That was a splendid kick!

A GIRL: Aren't his legs supple?

THE BOY [*dancing*]: The roof here is high, and there's plenty of room!¹

THE BRIDEGROOM [*going to his FATHER who is talking to some friends. Pulling at his sleeve, he whimpers*]:
Father, she *won't* – she's terribly stubborn.

THE FATHER: What won't she do?

THE BRIDEGROOM: She's locked herself in!

THE FATHER: Well, you must try to find the key, then.

THE BRIDEGROOM: I don't know how.

THE FATHER: What a ninny you are!
[*He turns to his friends. The BRIDEGROOM drifts across the yard.*]

A YOUTH [*coming from behind the house*]: *Now* things are going to get lively, girls –
Peer Gynt's turned up!

ASLAK [*who has just entered*]: Who invited him?

THE MASTER OF CEREMONIES: No one.
[*He goes to the house.*]

ASLAK [*to the girls*]: If he speaks to you, girls, just pretend not to hear him.

A GIRL [*to the others*]: No, no, let's make out that we can't even see him!

---

1. In the open air not even the rafters can stop him.

PEER GYNT [*coming in, alert and eager. He stands in front of the group and claps his hands*]:

Which is the sprightliest girl of the lot of you?

A GIRL [*whom he has approached*]:

Not me!

ANOTHER [*likewise*]: Nor me.

A THIRD:               And not me either.

PEER GYNT [*to a fourth*]: Then *you*'ll do, till somebody better turns up.

THE GIRL: I haven't got time.

PEER GYNT [*to a fifth*]:      Then you.

GIRL [*as she goes*]:                I'm off home!

PEER GYNT: Tonight? Why, you must be out of your senses!

ASLAK [*after a moment, softly*]: Look, Peer, she's dancing with that old gaffer.

PEER GYNT [*turning quickly to an older man*]: Where are the single girls?

THE MAN [*moving away*]: Go out and find them!

    [PEER GYNT *is suddenly subdued; he glances shyly and surreptitiously at the crowd. They all watch him, but no one speaks. He approaches another group, but wherever he turns there is silence. When he turns away, they look after him and smile.*]

PEER GYNT [*under his breath*]: Thoughts, smiles, and glances that pierce me like gimlets –

they jar like a file when it grates on a saw-blade.

    [*He slinks along the fence.* SOLVEIG,[1] *with little* HELGA *holding her hand, comes into the yard followed by her* PARENTS.]

A MAN [*to another, close to* PEER GYNT]: Look, it's the newcomers.

    1. The Norwegian pronunciation of Solveig is *Sohl*-vey.

THE OTHER:     They're from the West, aren't they?

THE FIRST MAN:
  Yes, they're from Hedal.[1]

THE OTHER:             Ah yes, of course.

PEER GYNT [*standing in front of the newcomers, pointing to*
     SOLVEIG, *he speaks to the man*]:
  May I dance with your daughter?

THE FATHER [*stopping*]:          Certainly; first though
  we must go in and pay our respects to our hosts.
          [*They go in.*]

THE MASTER OF CEREMONIES [*to* PEER GYNT, *offering
     him a drink*]:
  Since you've come here, you might just as well wet your
     whistle!

PEER GYNT [*following them with his eyes*]: Thanks, I'll be
  dancing – I'm not really thirsty.
          [THE MASTER OF CEREMONIES *leaves him*;
          PEER GYNT *looks towards the house and smiles.*]
  How lovely! I've never seen anyone like her –
  with her eyes on the ground and her little white apron,
  and the way she kept hold of her mother's skirts,
  and carried her prayerbook wrapped in a kerchief. . . .
  I must see her again.
          [*He goes towards the house.*]

A YOUTH [*coming out with several others*]:
                    Why, Peer, are you leaving
  the party already?

PEER GYNT:     No no!

THE YOUTH:          Then you're going
  the wrong way!

1. Although there is a Hedal in the Gudbrandsdal, since the newcomers
are 'from the West', Ibsen is probably thinking of Hedal near Lake Sprillen
in Valdres.

[*Taking him by the shoulders and turning him round*]

PEER GYNT: Let me pass!

THE YOUTH: Are you frightened of Aslak?

PEER GYNT: Me? Frightened?

THE YOUTH: Remember what happened at Lundë!
[*The group laughs and goes down to join the dancing.*]

SOLVEIG [*at the door*]: You're surely the boy who was wanting to dance?

PEER GYNT: Why yes, of course. Can't you see that I am?
[*Taking her hand*]
Come along.

SOLVEIG: Not too far, mother says.

PEER GYNT: 'Mother says – mother says'? Why, were you born yesterday?

SOLVEIG: You're laughing at me.

PEER GYNT: You're almost a baby – are you grown up?

SOLVEIG: I was confirmed last spring.

PEER GYNT: Tell me your name. We can talk better then.

SOLVEIG: My name is Solveig. And what is *your* name?

PEER GYNT: Peer Gynt.

SOLVEIG [*drawing her hand away*]: Oh, my goodness –

PEER GYNT: What's wrong now?

SOLVEIG: My garter's come loose, I must tie it again.
[*She goes.*]

THE BRIDEGROOM [*tugging at his mother*]: Mother, she won't . . .!

HIS MOTHER:  She won't? Won't what?

THE BRIDEGROOM:
She won't, Mother.

HIS MOTHER:  What?

THE BRIDEGROOM:  Unlock the door.

HIS FATHER [*under his breath, angrily*]: Oh, you're only fit
to be kept in a stable!

HIS MOTHER: Don't scold him, poor darling, he'll soon be
all right.
[*They go.*]

A YOUTH [*coming from among the dancers, with a crowd of
others*]:
Some brandy, Peer?

PEER GYNT:  No.

THE YOUTH:  Not even a drop?

PEER GYNT [*looking at him gloomily*]:
Why, have you got any?

THE YOUTH:  Ah, that's as may be.
[*He pulls out a pocket-flask and drinks.*]
Mm, that's got a bit of a bite to it! Well?

PEER GYNT: Let me try.
[*He drinks.*]

A SECOND YOUTH:  Good! and now try a swig
out of mine.

PEER GYNT: No.

THE SECOND YOUTH: Come along. What a milksop you
are!
Drink up, Peer!

PEER GYNT:  All right then, I'll just have a drop.
[*He drinks again.*]

A GIRL [*under her breath*]:
Oh, come on, let's go.

PEER GYNT:  Are you scared of me, girl?

47

A THIRD YOUTH:
  Who wouldn't be frightened of you?
A FOURTH:                          Why, at Lundë
  you left us no doubts about what you can do!
PEER GYNT: I can do more than that if I once lose my
    temper!
FIRST YOUTH [*whispering*]:
  We're getting him going!
SEVERAL [ *forming a ring round him*]:
                          Well, tell us! Yes, tell us!
  What can you do?
PEER GYNT:        Tomorrow . . .
OTHERS:                      No, now!
A GIRL: Peer, can you cast spells?
PEER GYNT:                    I can call up the devil!
A MAN: My Granny could do that before I was born!
PEER GYNT: That's a lie! I can do things that nobody else
    can.
  There was one time I conjured him into a nutshell.
  Well, there was a wormhole –
SEVERAL [*laughing*]:          Ah yes, we guessed that!
PEER GYNT: He cursed and he wept, and he promised to
    give me . . .
  well – all sorts of things –
ONE OF THE CROWD:     But you made him crawl in?
PEER GYNT: I did. Then I stopped up the hole with a
    plug.
  Oh, if only you'd heard how he roared and complained!
A GIRL: Fancy that!
PEER GYNT:        It was just like a bumble-bee buzzing.
THE GIRL: And have you still got him – sealed up in the
    nutshell?
PEER GYNT: Oh no, the devil got clean away;

it's all *his* fault that the smith doesn't like me.

A YOUTH:
How is that?

PEER GYNT: Well, I went to the smithy and asked him
if he'd smash up that nutshell to powder for me.
He said 'yes', and I put the thing down on the anvil.
But Aslak, from swinging that hammer all day,
has grown to be so heavy-handed, you know –

A VOICE FROM THE CROWD:
Did he smash up the devil?

PEER GYNT: He struck like a man;
but the devil took care of himself – like a flash
he'd split open the wall and the roof, and was out!

SEVERAL:
But the smith –?

PEER GYNT: He just stood there with blistered fingers,
and since that day, we've never been friends.

    [*General laughter.*]

SOME VOICES:
That's a wonderful yarn!

OTHERS:
                    Yes, it's one of his best!

PEER GYNT: What? Do you think I was making it up?

A MAN: No, I'm certain you weren't – for I've heard it
    before
from my grandad –[1]

PEER GYNT: You liar! It happened to *me*!

THE MAN: Well, that's all that matters, then!

PEER GYNT [*with a toss of his head*]: Hey, I can ride
clean through the air on the finest of horses.
*I* can do lots of things, I can. You'll see!

    1. This story, like that of Gudbrand Glesnë and the buck, appears in
Asbjørnsen.

[*More guffaws.*]

ONE OF THE CROWD:
Ride through the air, Peer!

MANY VOICES:              Yes, dear Peer Gynt, do!

PEER GYNT: There's no need to labour so hard to per-
suade me;
I'll ride high above all your heads like a storm
and the whole of the parish will fall at my feet!

AN OLDER MAN:
Now he's gone right off his head!

ANOTHER:                   What a numskull!

A THIRD: You braggart!

A FOURTH:           You liar!

PEER GYNT [*threatening them*]:    Just wait, and you'll see!

A MAN [*half drunk*]: Yes, wait – and you'll get your jacket
dusted!

MANY VOICES: A good sound thrashing! A lovely black
eye!

[*The crowd disperses, the older men angry, the younger
laughing and jeering.*]

THE BRIDEGROOM [*sidling up to him*]: Peer, is it true you
can ride through the air?

PEER GYNT [*curtly*]: Yes Mads, every word. I'm the boy,
you can bet!

THE BRIDEGROOM: And do you possess the Invisible
Cloak?

PEER GYNT: The Hat, do you mean? Yes, I've got that as
well.

[*He turns away;* SOLVEIG *comes across the yard
hand-in-hand with* HELGA.]

PEER GYNT [*going to them; more cheerfully*]: Solveig! Oh,
I'm so glad that you've come!

[*Grasping her wrists*]

Now I shall swing you round handsomely!

SOLVEIG:

Let me go!

PEER GYNT: No, why should I?

SOLVEIG:               Because you're so wild!

PEER GYNT: The reindeer's wild when the summer's
    coming!

Come on, my girl, and don't be sulky.

SOLVEIG [drawing her arm away]:

I dare not.

PEER GYNT: Why not, then?

SOLVEIG:               Because you've been drink-
    ing.

    [She goes away with HELGA.]

PEER GYNT: Oh, if I'd only taken my claspknife

and jabbed it right through them – one and all!

THE BRIDEGROOM [nudging him with his elbow]: Can't you
    help me to get to the bride?

PEER GYNT [absently]:

The bride? Where's she?

THE BRIDEGROOM:     In the outhouse.

PEER GYNT:                     Well!

THE BRIDEGROOM: Oh listen, Peer Gynt, you might have
    a try.

PEER GYNT: No, you must manage without me to help
    you.

    [A thought strikes him, and he asks, softly and sharply]

In the outhouse? Ingrid?

    [He goes to SOLVEIG.]

              Have you changed your mind?

    [SOLVEIG tries to go, but he stands in her way.]

You're ashamed of me – I look like a tramp.

SOLVEIG: Oh no, you don't. That isn't true.

PEER GYNT: It is. And what's more, I've had too much to
drink –

but that was for spite, when you hurt me. So come.

SOLVEIG: If I wanted to, I shouldn't dare.

PEER GYNT: What are you frightened of?

SOLVEIG:                                             Father, mostly.

PEER GYNT: Your father? Ah yes – is he one of the quiet
ones?

A psalm-singer, is he? Well, answer me, then.

SOLVEIG: What can I say?

PEER GYNT:                       Is your father strait-laced?

And so are you and your mother, aren't you?

Well, answer me, can't you?

SOLVEIG:                            Please let me go.

PEER GYNT: No!

[*Quietly, but still harsh and threatening*]

                   You know I can turn myself into a troll?

At midnight tonight I shall be at your bedside,

so when you hear something that hisses and splutters

you mustn't go telling yourself it's the cat,

for it'll be me! And I'll drink up your blood –

and your little sister I'll gobble up, too.

Oh yes, let me tell you, at night I'm a werewolf –

I'll bite you all over your sides and your back!

[*Changing his tone and begging her desperately*]

Dance with me, Solveig!

SOLVEIG [*looking at him miserably*]: No, now you've been
horrid!

[*She goes into the house.*]

THE BRIDEGROOM [*drifting in again*]:

I'll give you an ox if you'll help me!

PEER GYNT                                    Come on!

[*They go behind the house. Meanwhile a big crowd,*

*most of them drunk, comes from the dancing. There is
noise and confusion.* SOLVEIG, HELGA, *and their*
PARENTS *come out of the door, with a few older
people.*]

THE MASTER OF CEREMONIES [*to* ASLAK, *who is leading
the crowd*]:
  Now go easy!

ASLAK [*pulling his jacket off*]: No, it's got to be settled –
either Peer Gynt or I is in for a thrashing![1]

SEVERAL VOICES:
  Let them fight it out!

OTHERS:             No, let them argue!

ASLAK: We'll settle with fists, I've got no use for words.

SOLVEIG'S FATHER:
  Control yourself, man!

HELGA:            Will they beat him, mother?

A YOUTH: Let's tease him about all his lying, instead.

ANOTHER:
  Throw him out of the party!

A THIRD:         And spit in his eye!

A FOURTH [*to Aslak*]:
  Are you backing out?

ASLAK [*throwing his jacket aside*]: I'll murder the oaf!

SOLVEIG'S MOTHER [*to* SOLVEIG]: Now you can see
  what they think of the blockhead.

ÅSE [*coming in with a stick in her hand*]: Is that son of mine
  here? Well, he's in for a beating!
  Ooh! How soundly I'm going to thump him!

ASLAK [*rolling up his sleeves*]: A cudgel's too soft for a body
  like his!

SEVERAL VOICES:
  The blacksmith'll thrash him!

---

1. Literally 'must be bent to the hillside', that is 'made to bite the dust'.

OTHERS: Bash him!

ASLAK [*spitting on his hands and winking at* ÅSE]: Smash him!

ÅSE: What, smash my Peer? Just you see if you dare!
Old Åse here[1] has got teeth and claws.
Where is he?
[*Calling across the yard*]
Peer!

THE BRIDEGROOM [*coming running*]: Oh God in heaven!
Oh father – oh mother – do come!

HIS FATHER: What's the matter?

THE BRIDEGROOM:
Peer Gynt . . . oh, to think of it!

ÅSE [*with a scream*]: Ah! Have they murdered him?

THE BRIDEGROOM: No! Peer Gynt – look at him, there on the hillside!

MANY VOICES:
With the bride!

ÅSE [*letting her stick fall*]: Oh, the brute!

ASLAK [*in amazement*]: That's the steepest part!
My God! He can climb like a mountain goat!

THE BRIDEGROOM:
Mother! He's carrying her – like a pig!

ÅSE [*shaking her fist at* PEER]:
I hope you fall down!
[*With a scream of terror*]
Oh, mind where you're going!

INGRID'S FATHER [*coming out bareheaded and white with rage*]:
He's stolen the bride! Oh, I'll massacre him!

ÅSE: Oh no, don't you dare! Or may God strike me dead!

1. Literally 'Åse and I', an old-fashioned country expression.

# ACT TWO

*A high narrow mountain track. It is early morning.* PEER GYNT *hurries sullenly along the path;* INGRID, *still in some of her wedding finery, tries to hold him back.*

PEER GYNT: Go away!
INGRID [*weeping*]: Where can I go, after this?
PEER GYNT: Go where you like, for all I care!
INGRID [*wringing her hands*]:
How you've deceived me!
PEER GYNT: It's no good your whining –
now we must go our different ways.
INGRID: Sin – and again sin – binds us together.
PEER GYNT: Devil take all who would remind me –
and the devil take all women . . .
all but one. . . .
INGRID: And which one's that?
PEER GYNT: Not you, for certain.
INGRID: Then who is it?
PEER GYNT: Go away! Back where you came from –
back to your father!
INGRID: But my dearest . . .!
PEER GYNT: Shut up!
INGRID: You can't really mean
what you say.
PEER GYNT: I can and do!
INGRID: First you tempt me, and then you leave me!
PEER GYNT: Well, what else have you got to offer?
INGRID: The farm at Hægstad – and more besides.

PEER GYNT: Have you a prayerbook wrapped in your
    kerchief?
  Have you a gold plait that hangs down your back?
  Do you look modestly down at your apron?
  Do you hold on to your mother's skirt?
  *Do* you?
INGRID: No, but –
PEER GYNT:     Was it last spring
  that you were confirmed?
INGRID:     But listen, Peer –
PEER GYNT: Do you blush and lower your eyelids?
  Can you deny me when I beg?
INGRID: Lord! I think he's out of his mind!
PEER GYNT: Do a man's thoughts all grow holy
  when he sees you? Do they?
INGRID:     No, but –
PEER GYNT: Then what else is there that counts?
     [*He starts to go.*]
INGRID: You know that it's a hanging matter
  to desert me?
PEER GYNT:   Then so be it.
INGRID: I should bring you wealth and honour
  if you wed me –
PEER GYNT:     I've no right. . . .
INGRID [*bursting into tears*]:
  You enticed me!
PEER GYNT:     You were willing!
INGRID: I was wretched.
PEER GYNT:     I was mad.
INGRID: I shall make you pay for this!
PEER GYNT: Any price would be a bargain!
INGRID: Is your mind made up, then?
PEER GYNT:     Firmly!

INGRID: Very well! We'll see who wins!
　　　　[*She goes down the hill.*]
PEER GYNT [*is silent for a moment, then he cries out*]:
　　Devil take all who would remind me,
　　and the devil take all women!
INGRID [*turning her head and calling back mockingly*]:
　　All but *one.*
PEER GYNT: Yes, all but *one.*
　　　　[*They go their separate ways.*]

*

By a mountain lake surrounded by boggy moorland. A storm is
blowing up. ÅSE is peering desperately in all directions, calling
as she does so. SOLVEIG has difficulty in keeping pace with her.
Her PARENTS and HELGA are a little behind.


ÅSE [*tearing her hair and thrashing about with her arms*]:
　　The world, in its angry might, is against me!
　　The sky, the waters, the hateful mountains.
　　Mists from the skies roll down to mislead him,
　　the treacherous waters will take his life,
　　the mountains will kill him with landslide and chasm;
　　the people, too, are out for his life!
　　By God, they shall not! I cannot lose him!
　　Oh the fool – to be tempted so of the devil!
　　　　[*To* SOLVEIG]
　　But I can't believe such a thing could have happened!
　　He was always so full of lies and stories,
　　his greatest strength was in his tongue –
　　he never *did* anything in his life!
　　He – oh, I want to laugh and cry!

We clung together in want and sorrow –
for I must tell you, my husband drank,
roaming the district with foolish chatter,
wasting and trampling our wealth underfoot
while I sat at home with Little Peer. . . .
What could we do but try to forget?
I was too weak to face the truth –
it's a terrible thing to look fate in the face,
so you try to shrug your troubles away
and do your best to keep from thinking;
some try lies, and some try brandy,
but, ah, we took to fairy tales
of princes, trolls, enchanted beasts,
and stolen brides. . . . But who'd have thought
those devil's tales would stay with him?
>           [*Frightened again*]
What was that cry? Some goblin or gnome?
Peer! Peer! . . . Are you up there on the heights? –
>           [*She runs up a low hill and looks out over the water.
>           The others go to her.*]
Not a trace to be seen!

THE FATHER [*quietly*]:   It's worse for him.

ÅSE [*weeping*]: My little Peer! My poor lost lamb!

THE FATHER [*nodding gently*]:
That's true, he's lost.

ÅSE:                    Never say that!
He's very clever – there's no one like him!

THE FATHER: You foolish woman!

ÅSE:                    Yes, yes, I know;
I'm foolish, but my boy is fine!

THE FATHER [*always softly and with kindly eyes*]:
His heart is hardened, his soul is lost.

ÅSE [*distressed*]: No no! God could not be so cruel!

THE FATHER: Do you think he sighs at the weight of his sins?

ÅSE [*warmly*]: No . . . he can ride through the air on a reindeer!

THE MOTHER:
Lord! Are you mad?

THE FATHER: Woman, what are you saying?

ÅSE: There isn't a feat that's too hard for him –
you'll see – if only he lives to perform it!

THE FATHER: It would be better to see him hanged.

ÅSE [*with a scream*]: In Jesus' Name . . .!

THE FATHER: At the hangman's hands
perhaps his heart might turn to repentance.

ÅSE [*confused*]: You're driving me dizzy with all your talk!
We must find him!

THE FATHER: And save his soul –

THE MOTHER: – and his body!
If he's in the swamp, we must drag him out;
if the trolls have got him, we'll ring the bells.[1]

THE FATHER: Ah! Here's a track –

ÅSE: May God reward you
for helping me.

THE FATHER: It's my Christian duty.

ÅSE: So the rest were heathens – fie on them, then!
Not one of them would search with us.

THE FATHER:
They knew him too well.

ÅSE: He was too good for them.
[*Wringing her hands*]
And to think – to think that his life is in danger!

1. The sound of church bells was said to render the trolls powerless, as we see later in the Dovrë scene.

THE FATHER:
Here's a man's footprint!

ÅSE:                              Then we must follow.

THE FATHER: Spread out below the upland pastures!

[*He and his* WIFE *go on ahead.*]

SOLVEIG [*to* ÅSE]: Tell me some more.

ÅSE [*drying her eyes*]:                    About my son?

SOLVEIG: Yes. Everything.

ÅSE [*smiling and holding up her head*]: Everything? That
    would tire you.

SOLVEIG: You would be weary of the telling
    long before I should be tired of hearing.

*

*Low treeless heights below the high mountains. Tall peaks in the
distance. It is late in the day and the shadows are lengthening.*

PEER GYNT [*coming in at full speed and pausing on a slope*]:
    The crowd are after me – all the parish –
    all of them armed with sticks and guns,
    and the old man from Hægstad leads the pack, howling,
    Everyone knows that Peer Gynt's on the run!
    Here's something better than fighting the smith –
    this is life! Every limb is as strong as a bear's!
        [*He leaps up and down, striking out at the air.*]
    To hold back the torrent! To crush and to conquer!
    To shatter – to tear up a tree by the roots!
    Yes, this is life! It uplifts me and strengthens.
    The devil may take all my worthless lies!
        [*Three* UPLAND HERD-GIRLS[1] *run over the hill,*

1. The Norwegian word is *sæterjente*. Archer renders this as Sæter
Girls, which has led some stage producers, perhaps catching an overtone
from 'satyr', into making the girls into something supernatural. But a

*shouting and singing.*]

GIRLS: Trond of the Valfjeld! Bård and Kårë![1]
  Troll-pack, will you sleep in our arms?
PEER GYNT: Who are you calling to?
GIRLS:                              Trolls! To trolls!
FIRST GIRL:
  Trond! Be kind to me!
SECOND GIRL:          Bård! Be rough with me!
THIRD GIRL: All the beds in the hut are empty!
FIRST GIRL: Kindness is rough!
SECOND GIRL:                And roughness kind!
THIRD GIRL: For want of boys we play with trolls!
PEER GYNT:
  Where are your lads, then?
ALL THREE [*roaring with laughter*]:
                              Not free to come!
FIRST GIRL: Mine called me dearest, and nearest, too –
  then went and married a middle-aged widow!
SECOND GIRL: Mine met a gipsy-wench up in the North –
  now they're tramping the roads together.
THIRD GIRL: Mine put an end to our bastard brat –
  his head stands grinning now on a stake!
ALL THREE: Trond of the Valfjeld! Bård and Kårë!
  Troll-pack! Will you sleep in our arms?
PEER GYNT [*leaping into the midst of them*]: I'm a three-
        headed troll – just the one for three girls!
GIRLS: Are you man enough?

---

*sæter* is merely a high mountain pasture where the girls take the cattle in
the spring and stay with them, living in small mountain huts and making
cheese from the milk, till the snows threaten again. The girls are entirely
human, and very lonely.
  1. Trond of the Valfjeld was one of the trolls whom Peer Gynt outwitted
in Asbjørnsen's book. The names are pronounced Tron of the *Vahl*-fyel,
Bawrrd, and *Kaw*-ruh.

PEER GYNT: Just try me and see!

FIRST GIRL:
  To the hut – to the hut!

SECOND GIRL: We have drink!

PEER GYNT: Let it flow!

THIRD GIRL:
  It's Saturday night – not a bed will be empty!

SECOND GIRL [*kissing him*]:
  He glows and sparkles like red-hot steel!

THIRD GIRL [*also kissing him*]:
  Like the mountain trout[1] from the blackest pool!

PEER GYNT [*dancing with them*]:
  Dismal bodings and wanton thoughts –
  laughing eyes and a sob in the throat!

GIRLS [*singing and shouting, and cocking snooks at the mountain
      tops*]:
  Trond of the Valfjeld, Bård and Kårë!
  Troll-pack! Did you sleep in our arms?
      [*They dance over the hill with* PEER GYNT *between
      them.*]

\*

*Among the Rondë mountains. It is sunset, and all the surrounding
snow-covered peaks are gleaming.* PEER GYNT *comes in, wild
and distraught.*

PEER GYNT: Palace on palace is rising!
  See, how that gateway glitters!
  Stop! Will you stop! Now they're drifting
  farther and farther away!
  The cock on the weather-vane's spreading

  1. *Barneøjne* is literally 'babies'-eyes', an obsolete country name for
trout, presumably from the spots on their flanks.

his wings, as if he would hover. . . .
Now all is blue haze in the gorges
and the mountain is locked and barred.

What are those roots and branches
that spring from the clefts at the summit?
They are heroes, heron-footed. . . .
Now they, too, have faded to nothing.

A gleam like the bands of the rainbow
pierces my sight and my senses.
What is that distant chiming?
What weighs my eyelids down?
Ah, how my head is aching
as if circled with red-hot steel;
and I cannot remember what devil
has bound it around my forehead.

[*He sinks down.*]

That ride on the ridge at Gjendin
was a tale – a damnable lie.
Climbing the steepest hillside
with the bride . . . drunk a night and a day . . .
hunting with kites and with falcons . . .
threatened by trolls and their kinsfolk . . .
sporting with crazy women . . .
all a lie – a damnable tale.

[*He stares upwards for a while.*]

There soar two tawny eagles –
and wild geese fly to the Southlands,
while here I stumble and trudge
knee-deep in quagmire and slime.

[*Springing up*]

I will join them – washing my sins clean
in a stream of the keenest wind!
I will soar – I will plunge myself deep

in that shining baptismal font.
I will fly over upland meadows;
I will ride where my fancy takes me –
far over salty seas,
high above Engelland's princes.
Yes, you may stare, you maidens,
but your waiting is all in vain
for my steed will never return –
Well – maybe I might swoop down. . . .
    Where are they – my tawny eagles?
I think the devil has taken them!
    Look, a gable-end is rising –
growing higher, stone by stone,
raising itself from the rubble.
There stands the door – wide open. . . .
Ah, but I know it now,
it's Grandfather's farm, newly built!
There are no rags now in the windows,
no fencing ready to fall.
Lights blaze from every casement
and there, in the great hall, is feasting.
    Hark, there's the Provost tapping
his knife-edge against his glass;
the Captain has flung his bottle
and shattered the mirror in pieces!
Let them waste and let them squander –
Mother, hush! there's plenty to spare.
Rich Jon Gynt holds revel;
hurrah for the house of Gynt!
What is this movement and bustle –
this shouting? Ah, it's the Captain –
he calls for his host's young son!
There! the Provost is drinking my health!

Go in, Peer Gynt – hear their judgement,
it rings out in song and acclaim.
Peer Gynt, you have sprung from greatness,
and to greatness shall you attain!

> [*He springs forward, but runs his head full-tilt into a
> rock. He falls and lies still.*[1]]

*

*A hillside, with tall trees sighing in the wind. Stars twinkle
through the branches, and birds sing in the tree-tops. A* WOMAN
IN GREEN *comes over the slope:* PEER GYNT *follows her, per-
orming all sorts of lovesick antics.*

THE WOMAN IN GREEN [*stopping and turning round*]:
   Is that true?
PEER GYNT [*drawing a finger across his throat*]:
               It's as true as that my name is Peer.
   As true as that you are a beautiful woman.
   Will you take me? You'll soon learn how kind I can be –
   I shall never expect you to weave or to spin;
   meat you shall eat till you're ready to burst.
   I'll never drag you about by your hair –
THE WOMAN: Nor beat me, either?
PEER GYNT:                      Now is it likely?
   We sons of kings don't beat our women.
THE WOMAN:
   A king's son?
PEER GYNT:  Yes.
THE WOMAN:      I'm the Dovrë King's daughter.
PEER GYNT: Is that so? Well, well – we were made for
      each other!

   1. All that happens to Peer from here to the end of the Act could be
delirium following this blow on the head.

THE WOMAN: My father's palace is deep in the mountains.

PEER GYNT: My mother's is bigger than his, I can tell you.

THE WOMAN: Do you know my father? His name is King Brosë.

PEER GYNT: Do you know my mother? Her name is Queen Åse.

THE WOMAN: When my father is angry, the mountains crumble!

PEER GYNT: They shake if my mother only scolds!

THE WOMAN: My father can kick the highest rafters.[1]

PEER GYNT: My mother can ride through the swiftest flood.[2]

THE WOMAN: Have you other garments besides those rags?

PEER GYNT: Ah, wait till you see my Sunday-best!

THE WOMAN: My weekday clothes are of silk and gold.

PEER GYNT: They look to me more like grasses and straw.

THE WOMAN: Ah, that's a thing that you'll have to get used to –
it's a custom among us Rondë folk
that everything has a double shape.
Now, when you come to my father's palace,
you'll probably think that you're in the ugliest
heap of old rubbish you ever saw!

PEER GYNT: Well now, it's exactly the same with us:
our gold you would take for rust and mildew,
and you'd probably think that our glittering windows
were merely bundles of rags and old stockings.

THE WOMAN: Black looks like white, and ugly like fair.

---

1. She is boasting of his prowess in the Halling.
2. She did so in the first scene – on Peer's back.

PEER GYNT: Big looks like little, and dirty like clean.

THE WOMAN [*falling on his neck*]: Oh, Peer, I can see we shall get on together!

PEER GYNT: Like the leg to the breeches, the hair to the comb.

THE WOMAN [*calling over the hill*]:

My steed! My steed! My wedding steed!

> [*A gigantic pig comes running up, with a rope's-end for a bridle and an old sack for a saddle.* PEER GYNT *swings himself up and places the* WOMAN IN GREEN *in front of him.*]

PEER GYNT: Hoop-la! We'll gallop through Rondë's gates!

Gee-up, gee-up, my noble charger!

THE WOMAN [*affectionately*]: And just now I was feeling so lonely and sad!

Well, you never can tell what may happen to you!

PEER GYNT [*beating the pig till it trots off*]: Great folk may be known by the mounts that they ride.

*

*The royal hall of the* OLD MAN OF THE DOVRË.[1] *There is a great crowd of troll* COURTIERS, GNOMES *and* GOBLINS. *The* OLD MAN *sits on his throne, with crown and sceptre, surrounded by his children and relatives.* PEER GYNT *stands before him. There is a tremendous uproar in the hall.*

1. Perhaps because we are more familiar with Grieg's incidental music than with Ibsen's text, he is usually called the Dovrë King, from 'The Hall of the Mountain King'; but Ibsen uses the word 'king' only in the boasting of the Woman in Green, just as Peer claims that his mother is 'Queen' Åse. Everywhere else, he uses the word '*Gubbe*' which is cognate with our 'Gaffer'. He took the name *Dovregubbe* from Hans Andersen's story *Elvehøi* (The Fairy Hill), a tale which, from the way it pokes fun at Norwegian Nationalism, must have appealed particularly to Ibsen.

TROLL COURTIERS: Kill him! The Christian's son has deceived
the fairest daughter of our ruler!

A YOUNG TROLL:
Let me cut off his fingers!

ANOTHER:                              Let me tear out his hair!

A TROLL MAIDEN: Oooh-ah! Let me bite his bottom!

A TROLL WITCH [*with a ladle*]: Shall he be boiled to a
broth in brine?

ANOTHER WITCH [*with a cleaver*]: Spitted and roasted? Or
stewed in a cauldron?

THE OLD MAN: Keep cool now – ice-cool![1]
    [*Beckoning his Courtiers about him*]
                              We mustn't show off!
Just lately we haven't been doing too well,
and we don't know whether we'll prosper or perish
so we mustn't turn down any possible help.
Besides, this young fellow is almost unblemished,
and he's quite well built – as far as we know.
It's true he has only a single head,
but then, my daughter has only one.
Three-headed trolls have gone right out of fashion,
and you don't see all *that* many two-headed ones –
and their heads, when you *do* see them, aren't up to much.
    [*To* PEER]
Well now, I gather you're after my daughter?

PEER GYNT: Your daughter, yes – and your kingdom as
dowry.

OLD MAN: You can have one half of it while I'm alive;
the rest will come to you when I snuff out.

---

1. Literally 'Ice-water in the blood!' The more usual Norwegian expression is 'Cold water in the blood!'. The OLD MAN is using a superlative.

PEER GYNT: Yes, that's all right.

OLD MAN: Just a moment, my boy—
you'll have to make a few promises too.
If you break even one of them – everything's off,
and you'll never get out of here alive!
First, you must promise to wipe from your mind
everything outside the confines of Rondë –
shun the day, and its deeds, and whatever is sunlit.

PEER GYNT: When once I'm a king, then that shouldn't
be hard.

OLD MAN: Next, I want to find out just how clever you
are.

    [*He rises from his seat.*]

THE OLDEST TROLL COURTIER [*to* PEER GYNT]:
Let's see if you've got a wisdom-tooth
that can crack the nut of the Old Man's riddle.

OLD MAN: What is the difference between trolls and men?

PEER GYNT: As far as *I* can see – none at all.
Big trolls will roast you, and little trolls claw you;
and we'd be the same – if only we dared.

OLD MAN: True; in that, and in other respects, we're
alike.
But morning is morning and evening is evening,
and one huge difference stands between us. . . .
I'll tell you, now, what that difference is:
Outside among men, where the skies are bright,
there's a saying 'Man, to thyself be true';
but here among trolls, the saying runs:
'Troll, to thyself be – *enough.*'

COURTIER: Well? Do you get it?

PEER GYNT: I'm still a bit hazy. . . .

OLD MAN: 'Enough', my son! That shattering word
of Power must be your battle-cry.

PEER GYNT [*scratching his head*]:
But –?

OLD MAN: It *must*, if you're to be master here.

PEER GYNT: All right then, damn it; things might be
worse.

OLD MAN: Next, you must learn to appreciate
our simple homely way of living.[1]
[*He beckons, and two pig-faced trolls in white night-
caps, etc., bring food and drink.*]
Our cows give us cakes, and our oxen, ale;
never mind if the taste is sweet or bitter,
the point you must always bear in mind
is that all of it's genuinely home-made!

PEER GYNT [*pushing it away*]: The devil take your home-
made brew;
I'll never get used to your country's ways.

OLD MAN: The bowl goes with it, and that is gold.
Who owns the bowl shall have my daughter.

PEER GYNT [*thoughtfully*]: It's written 'Thou shalt subdue
thy nature' –
and the drink, after all, may not prove too sour.
Here goes!
[*He drinks.*]

OLD MAN: There! That was wisely spoken.
Did you spit?

PEER GYNT: Merely from force of habit.

OLD MAN: Next, you must throw off your Christian
clothes.
You must realize, it's our boast in Dovrë
that everything is mountain-made;
we've nothing here that comes from the valleys

1. Ibsen is satirizing the 'folksy' ultra-Nationalists of his day, and their
obsession with peasant crafts.

but the silken bows at the tips of our tails.

PEER GYNT [*angrily*]:
I haven't a tail!

OLD MAN: But you *shall* have one!
Steward, fix on him my Sunday-best tail.

PEER GYNT: No, you don't! Are you making a beast out
of me?

OLD MAN: Don't come courting my girl with no tail on
your rump!

PEER GYNT: Turning men into beasts!

OLD MAN: No, my son, you're mistaken;
it simply makes you a courtly wooer.
You may wear a flame-coloured bow on the end,
and that's a mark of the highest honour.

PEER GYNT [*thoughtfully*]: They say that Man is no more
than dust . . .
and one *should* fit in with the local ways.
Fix away!

OLD MAN: Now you're being a sensible lad!

COURTIER: Let's see how well you can wag it and wave
it!

PEER GYNT [*sulkily*]: Hm. Now what else do you want
me to do?
I suppose I must give up my Christian faith?

OLD MAN: No, that you can willingly keep in peace –
faith is free, it carries no duty.
The signs by which you can tell a troll
are his *outward* appearance – the cut of his coat.
Once we're agreed about customs and clothes,
you're free to *believe* things that we find revolting.

PEER GYNT: You're really – in spite of your many con-
ditions –
a more rational chap than I ever expected!

OLD MAN: My son, we trolls aren't as black as we're
painted –
that's another difference between us and you!
Well, that ends the serious part of our meeting,
now let us feast our eyes and ears.
Music, ho! Girls! Let the Dovrë harp sound!
Dancing-girls, hi! Tread the Dovrë hall's floor!
[*Music and a dance.*]
OLD MAN: What do you think of it?
PEER GYNT: Think of it? Well . . .
OLD MAN: You can speak quite frankly. What do you
see?
PEER GYNT: Something quite unbelievably ugly –
a bell-cow who plucks with her hoof at a catgut
while a pig in short stockings cavorts to the noise!
COURTIERS: Eat him!
OLD MAN: Remember, his senses are human!
TROLL MAIDENS: Ugh! Gouge out his eyes and then tear
off his ears!
THE WOMAN IN GREEN [*weeping*]: Ow! *Must* we put up
with an insult like that
when my sister and I have been playing and dancing?
PEER GYNT: Aha, was it you? Well, you know, at a
banquet
you can make little jokes and there's no offence meant.
THE WOMAN:
A joke? Will you swear it?
PEER GYNT: The music and dancing
were charming – or else may the cat scratch my face.
OLD MAN: It's a curious thing about human nature
how it clings to men for so long a time!
Though in tussles with us, it's often wounded,
yet it quickly heals, with hardly a scar.

My son-in-law, now, is as yielding as any;
He willingly doffed his Christian breeches,
he willingly finished his bowl of ale,
he willingly tied on a tail to his bottom. . . .
So willing he was to do just as we told him
that I really began to believe the Old Adam
for once in a while had been kicked out of doors;
yet here it is, back – and top-dog once again!
Ah yes, my son, we must give you some treatment
to cure all this human nature of yours.

PEER GYNT: What will you do?

OLD MAN:                         Simply scratch your left eye
a little bit, so that you'll see askew,
yet you'll think what you see is exactly right;
next I'll cut out your right-hand window-pane –

PEER GYNT: You're drunk!

OLD MAN [*laying several sharp instruments on the table*]:
                         Here, you see, are the glazier's tools.[1]
You'll have to be blinkered, like any mad bull. . . .
And then you'll look on your bride as lovely,
and never again will your sight deceive you
with pigs that caper and cows with bells.

PEER GYNT: All that is simply the talk of a madman!

THE OLDEST COURTIER: No, it's the talk of the Old Man
    of Dovrë.
He is the wise one, it's you who are mad.

OLD MAN: Just think how much trouble and tribulation
you would then be rid of for good and all.
For, when you consider it, eyes are the source
of that bitter blistering flux called tears!

PEER GYNT: True enough . . . and the Good Book tells us

---

1. This operation on the eyes is another bit of Gudbrandsdal folk-lore;
Asbjørnsen records it among the stories of Berthe Tuppenhaug.

'If thine eye offend thee, pluck it out!' ...[1]
But tell me – how soon will my eyes recover
their human sight?

OLD MAN:                    Never again, my friend.

PEER GYNT: Is that so? Then I must say 'No thanks'.

OLD MAN: What else do you want, then?

PEER GYNT:                              To go away.

OLD MAN: One moment! Getting *in* here's simple,
    but Dovrë's gates don't open outwards.

PEER GYNT: You wouldn't keep me against my will?

OLD MAN: Now look, Prince Peer – just listen to reason:
    you'd make a fine troll! See! Doesn't he carry
    himself like a genuine troll already?
    Now – will you become one?

PEER GYNT:                          Of course I will!
    To gain a bride and a kingdom as well
    I'm ready to give up a certain amount. ...
    Yet ... there's a limit to everything.
    It's perfectly true I've accepted a tail,
    but I can undo what your courtier tied.
    I've cast off my breeks, they were tattered and old,
    but I could easily put them back:
    and certainly I should also be able
    to throw off this trollish way of life –
    it's easy to swear that a cow is a maiden,
    and a man can always go back on an oath. ...
    But to know that I'll never be free again –
    that I shouldn't die as an honest man
    but pass as a hill-troll all my life,
    knowing that 'there is no return',

1. Matthew 5:29. For once Peer gets his Biblical quotation right. Some
thirty lines later, the Old Man refers to the preceding verse: 'Whosoever
looketh on a woman to lust after her ...'.

as it says in the Bible – *that* makes you think –
and it's something I shall never agree to.

OLD MAN: Now, for my sins,[1] I'm getting annoyed!
This is a thing that I won't put up with.
Do you know who I am, you pale-faced[2] lout?
First, you've been far too free with my daughter –

PEER GYNT: That's a lie!

OLD MAN:                    – and you'll have to marry her.

PEER GYNT:
Do you dare to accuse me –?

OLD MAN:                    What? Can you deny
that you have desired her – lusted after her?

PEER GYNT [*with a snort*]: Oh, *that*! What the hell does a
thing like that matter?

OLD MAN: You human beings are all the same –
continually talking about your souls,
but only thinking of what you can grab!
So! You really think that desires don't matter?
Wait, and you'll very soon see for yourself!

THE WOMAN IN GREEN:
Before the year's out you'll be a father!

PEER GYNT:
Open the gates! Let me out!

OLD MAN:                    Then we'll send you
the brat in a goatskin.

PEER GYNT [*wiping his brow*]: I wish I could wake!

OLD MAN:
Will you have him sent to your father's palace?

---

1. Literally 'True, by my vice', a trollish perversion of the more usual
'True, by my virtue'.
2. Literally 'day-white', but the trolls' hatred of the daylight seems un-
translatable in English.

PEER GYNT:
   To the workhouse!
OLD MAN:            Just as you like, Prince Peer,
   it's up to you. But one thing's certain –
   what's done is done. But your offspring will *grow* –
   these bastard brats grow terribly fast!
PEER GYNT: Don't rush at things like an ox, Old
         Man!
   See reason, Girl! Let's come to terms.
   I must tell you, I'm neither a prince, nor rich,
   and however you weigh or measure me
   you'll find that you won't get a lot from the deal!
         [THE WOMAN IN GREEN *swoons and is carried out
         by troll handmaidens.*]
OLD MAN [*looks at him for a moment with contempt, then
         orders*]:
   Smash him to bits on the rocks, my sons!
YOUNG TROLLS: Oh, Papa, mayn't we first play at barn-
         owls and eagles?
   Or the wolf-game? Or grey-mouse and gleaming-eyed
         cat?
OLD MAN: All right, but be quick; I'm angry and tired.
         Good night!
         [*He goes.*]
PEER GYNT [*as the* YOUNG TROLLS *hunt him*]:
   You devil's spawn! Will you let me go!
         [*Trying to get up the chimney*]
YOUNG TROLLS: Goblins! Dwarfs! Bite him behind!
PEER GYNT: Ow!
         [*Trying to get down through the cellar-flap*]
YOUNG TROLLS: Stop all the holes up!
COURTIER:                            How the children
   enjoy their fun!

PEER GYNT [*struggling with a little troll who has his teeth fast in* PEER'*s ear*]: Let go, you beast!

COURTIER [*rapping* PEER *over the knuckles*]:
Show respect, you oaf, to a royal child!

PEER GYNT: There's a rat hole!
        [*Running to it*]

YOUNG TROLLS:                Plug it, gnomes!

PEER GYNT:
The old one was foul, but the youngsters are worse!

YOUNG TROLLS: Flay him!

PEER GYNT:                I wish I was small as a mouse!
        [*Running here and there*]

YOUNG TROLLS [*closing round him*]:
Bar his way! Bar his way!

PEER GYNT [*in tears*]:        Oh, if I was a louse!
        [*He falls.*]

YOUNG TROLLS: Now go for his eyes!

PEER GYNT [*buried under the trolls*]:        Help, mother! –
        they'll kill me!
        [*Distant church bells ring.*]

YOUNG TROLLS: Bells in the mountains! The Black
        Cassock's cows!
        [*The* TROLLS *flee shrieking in disorder. The Hall
        falls in and everything vanishes.*]

*

*Pitch darkness.* PEER GYNT *can be heard flailing and laying
        about him with a great branch.*

PEER GYNT:
Who are you? Answer!

A VOICE IN THE DARK: My Self!

PEER GYNT:                Make way, then!

THE VOICE: Go round about, Peer – there's room on the mountain.

PEER GYNT [*pulled up short as he tries to pass another way*]:
Who are *you*?

THE VOICE:     My Self. Can *you* say as much?

PEER GYNT: I can say what I like, and my sword can strike home,

look out for yourself! Hey! Stand from under!

King Saul slew his hundreds, Peer Gynt slew his thousands!

     [*Laying about him*]

Who *are* you?

THE VOICE:     My Self.

PEER GYNT:          I can do without

stupid answers like that, that don't tell me a thing!

*What* are you?

THE VOICE:     The Great Boyg.[1]

PEER GYNT:               Oh? Is that so?

The riddle was black, now it seems to be grey.

Out of my way, Boyg!

---

1. We are inclined to think of the Great Boyg as a well-known and ubiquitous monster like the Kraken, but in fact he is a troll who appears in the Gudbrandsdal stories of Peer Gynt – and then only once. In Asbjørn-sen's version he gives his name as 'The Great Boyg of Etnedal'; he is enormous, slippery, and unpleasant to touch. He blocked Peer's way to the mountain hut that he wanted to reach. Whichever way Peer turned, he ran into the clammy mass. Eventually he managed to find the creature's head (which somehow makes it smaller and less menacing than Ibsen's formless Thing), and fired three shots into it. They had no effect, and the surrounding hills were filled with laughter and jeering. In the end, Peer managed to outwit him, in the rather unconvincing way that these things are done in folk-legends.

The name should strictly be written *Bøjg* – but, like Archer, I have used this simpler form as being easier for an English-speaking reader to pro-nounce. It comes from the Norwegian word *bøje* – to bend (German – *biegen*), suggesting something crooked and sinuous, and also something that makes one change course.

THE VOICE:                 Go round about, Peer!

PEER GYNT:

No, I'll go straight through you!
  [*Hacking and slashing*]
                              He's down!
  [*He tries to go forward but always finds himself
  obstructed.*]
                              Are there others?

THE VOICE: The Boyg, Peer Gynt, the one and the only!
  The Boyg who was wounded – the Boyg who is whole;
  the Boyg who was slain – and the Boyg who's alive!

PEER GYNT [*throwing away the branch*]: My weapon's be-
    witched,[1] but I still have my fists.
      [*Hitting out*]

THE VOICE: Yes, trust to your fists and trust to your
    sinews –
  ho ho, Peer Gynt – then you'll come out on top!

PEER GYNT: Backwards or forwards it's just as far,
  out or in, it's just as narrow.
  He's here, he's there, he's all about me!
  When I'm sure that I'm out, then I'm back in the middle!
  What's your name? Let me see you! What sort of thing
    *are* you?

THE VOICE: The Boyg.

PEER GYNT [*groping about*]: Neither dead nor alive . . .
    mist . . . and slime.
  Shapeless, too . . . it's like running into
  a nest of sleepy growling bears.
      [*Shouting*]
  Hit back at me!

THE VOICE:             The Boyg's no fool!

PEER GYNT: Hit out!

                1. Literally 'troll-smeared'.

79

THE VOICE: Not the Boyg!

PEER GYNT: Hit out! You shall!

THE VOICE: The Great Boyg conquers without a blow!

PEER GYNT: If only there were a gnome to goad me –
   if only there were a yearling troll!
   Just something to fight against! Here there's nothing.
   He's snoring now! Boyg!

THE VOICE: Well?

PEER GYNT: Use your strength!

THE VOICE: The Great Boyg conquers by gentleness.

PEER GYNT [*biting his own arms and hands*]: Let fangs and
      talons tear my flesh –
   I must see a drop of my own blood flowing!
      [*There is a sound like the beating of great birds'
      wings.*]

BIRDS' CRIES: Is he coming, Boyg?

THE VOICE: Yes. Step by step.

BIRDS' CRIES: Sisters from far off, fly hither to join
   us!

PEER GYNT: Girl, be quick if you mean to save me!
   Don't just hang your head and lower your eyes!
   Your prayerbook! Throw it straight in his face!

BIRDS' CRIES:
   He's failing!

THE VOICE: We've got him!

BIRDS' CRIES: Sisters, come quickly!

PEER GYNT: Life is too costly, if I must pay
   with an hour of torment such as this!
      [*He sinks down.*]

BIRDS' CRIES: Boyg – he is falling! Seize him, seize
   him!
      [*Church bells and the chanting of psalms are heard in
      the distance.*]

THE VOICE [*speaking with a gasp, as he shrinks to nothing*]:
  He was too strong. There were women behind him.

*

*Sunrise. On the hillside in front of Åse's upland hut.[1] The door*
*is barred and everything is still and empty.* PEER GYNT *lies*
*asleep outside the wall.*

PEER GYNT [*waking, and looking round with dull and listless*
    *eyes. He spits*]:
  If only I had a pickled herring!
      [*He spits again, and as he does so, he sees* HELGA
      *coming up with a basket of food.*]
  Ah, *you* here, Little'un? What do you want?
HELGA: Well, Solveig –
PEER GYNT [*jumping up*]: Where is she?
HELGA:                              Behind the hut.
SOLVEIG [*from her hiding-place*]:
  If you come any nearer, I'll run away.
PEER GYNT [*standing still*]:
  Are you afraid I shall carry *you* off?
SOLVEIG: For shame!
PEER GYNT: Do you know where I spent last night?
  The Old Man of the Dovrë's daughter
  was buzzing round me like a horsefly!
SOLVEIG: Then it's just as well that the bells were rung.
PEER GYNT: Ah, but Peer Gynt isn't the boy to get caught.
  What do you say?
HELGA [*in tears*]:      Oh, she's running away!
      [*Running after her*]
  Wait for me!

  1. This is not at the farm where the play opened, but on Åse's *sæter*, which
  would be deserted at this time of year, and so an excellent place for Peer
  to lie hidden.

PEER GYNT [*catching her by the arm*]: Just look what I've
    got in my pocket –
  a big silver button. I'll give it to you
  if you'll only speak up for me.
HELGA:                  No, let me go.
PEER GYNT: Here it is.
HELGA:              Let me go. I've left you the basket.
PEER GYNT:
  God help you, if –
HELGA:          You're frightening me!
PEER GYNT [*quietly, as he lets her go*]:
    No, I only meant – ask her not to forget me. . . .
      [HELGA *runs away.*]

# ACT THREE

*In the depths of a pine forest. It is a grey autumn day with snow falling.* PEER GYNT *is in his shirtsleeves, felling timber for building.*

PEER GYNT [*chopping at a great fir tree with twisted branches*]:
Oh yes, you're tough, you stubborn old man,
but that won't help you – you're coming down!
    [*Chopping again*]
I know that you're wearing a coat of mail,
but I shall hack through it, however tough.
Ah yes, you may well shake your twisted arms –
no doubt you're feeling indignant and angry,
but all the same, you must bend the knee!
    [*He breaks off suddenly in disgust.*]
What lies! This is only an ancient tree.
All lies – not a knight in armour at all,
but only a fir tree with wrinkled bark.
It's hard enough work to chop down trees,
but chopping and dreaming together's the devil!
I must stop it – this dreaming the whole day long,
going about with my head in the clouds.
You're an outlaw, my boy – forced to hide in the
    forest!
    [*He chops energetically for a while.*]
An outlaw, yes – up here there's no mother
to lay your table and bring you food.
If you want to eat, you must get it yourself –
finding it raw, in the stream and the forest.

You must forage for sticks to kindle your fire;
you must fetch and carry, and fend for yourself.
If you need warm clothes, you must skin a deer;
if you'd build a house, you must break the stones,
felling the trees for its wooden walls
and hauling them down on your back to the clearing.

[*Letting the axe fall, he stares in front of him.*]
I'll build a beauty! High on the roof ridge
I'll put a tower with a weather-vane.
At the gable-end I'll carve a mermaid,
shaped like a fish from the navel down.
The vane and the latches shall all be brass;
I must try to get window-panes as well –
so that strangers will wonder what it can be
that shines so bright on the distant hill!

[*He laughs bitterly.*]
There I go again – lying like hell!
You're an outlaw, my lad!

[*Chopping fiercely*]
                              A hut thatched with bark
will be shelter enough from the rain and frost.

[*Looking up at the tree*]
He's beginning to fall! Yes, only a push,
and then, with a crash he'll measure his length
while all the swarming undergrowth shudders.

[*He sets to work lopping the branches. Then suddenly,
with uplifted axe, he stops to listen.*]
There's somebody after me! Ah, is that you,
you old man from Hægstad, slinking about?

[*He hides, peeping out from behind the tree.*]
A boy . . . and alone. He seems afraid.
He's looking about him. What's that he's hiding
under his jacket? A sickle! He stops . . .

looks round . . . lays his hand on a log. . . .
Now what? Why does he brace himself?
Ugh! He can't have chopped a finger off!
Chopped it clean off! He bleeds like a pig!
Now he's running away, with his hand in a cloth.
    [*He gets up.*]
That was madness! A finger won't grow again!
He chopped it clean off – no one made him do it.
Aha, now I see. . . . That's the only way
that he can get out of serving the King.
That's it. They'd have sent him off to the war,
and the lad had to have an excuse, you see.
But to chop . . . to lose it for ever . . .
I might think of it – wish for it – want it badly. . . .
But to *do* it. . . . That's something I *can't* understand!
    [*Shaking his head a little, he goes on with his work.*]


\*


*A room in Åse's house. Everything is in disorder: the closet is
standing open, and clothes are scattered everywhere. A cat is on
the bed. ÅSE and a NEIGHBOUR are busy trying to collect things
and put them in order.*


ÅSE [*running across the room*]:
    Kari – one minute –
KARI:                        What is it?
ÅSE [*running back*]:                  Tell me
    where's my – where's – tell me, where can I find –?
    What am I looking for? Oh, I'm so stupid!
    Yes, where's the key to the chest?
KARI:                              In the keyhole.
ÅSE: What's all that rumbling?

KARI:                              That's the last load
being carted to Hægstad.[1]

ÅSE:                              If only they'd cart
me out too, for good, in a long black box.
Oh, what poor creatures like us have to suffer.
Merciful God! The whole house has been emptied –
What Hægstad has left, the bailiff has taken;
not even the clothes off my back have been left me.
Oh shame – shame on those who could give such a
       verdict!

       [*She sits on the edge of the bed.*]

The old man was harsh, but the law was harsher,
the farm and the land are gone now for ever.
With Peer away, I had no one to turn to –
I had no help, and I got no mercy.

KARI: You may stay in this house for the rest of your days.

ÅSE: Yes, the cat and I – eating charity-bread!

KARI: God help you, old mother, your Peer's cost you
       dear!

ÅSE: My Peer? Why, you must be out of your mind!
Ingrid came back safe and sound in the end.
They'd have done better to blame the Devil –
he was the culprit, and nobody else,
the ugly brute, when he tempted my boy.

KARI: Hadn't I better send for the Parson?
You may be more ill than ever you think.

ÅSE: The Parson? Perhaps that might be best.

       [*Getting up*]

But I *can't*! Oh God, I'm the boy's own mother –
I have to help him – it's only my duty.

---

1. As a punishment for abducting Ingrid, most of Peer's possessions
have gone to her father; the rest, as appears a few lines later, are forfeit to
the law.

I'll do what I can, since the others have failed him.
They've left him this jacket – I mean to patch it.
If only I'd dared to keep back the fur rug!
Where are the stockings?

KARI:                     Down there with the rubbish.

ÅSE [*rummaging about*]: Look what I've found! Well well,
    if it isn't

his old casting-ladle! He used to play, Kari,
at being a moulder of buttons;[1] he'd melt,
and he'd mould, and he'd stamp. . . . I remember one
    day

when my husband had company, in came the boy
asking his father to give him some tin.
'Not tin,' answered Jon, 'but King Christian's coin!
Silver! To show you're the son of Jon Gynt!'
My Jon was drunk, may God forgive him,
and tin and gold were alike to him. . . .
Here are the stockings – full of holes!
I must darn them, Kari.

KARI:                     And not before time!

ÅSE: And when I've done that, I must go to bed –
    I feel so wretched and weak and ill.

        [*Joyfully*]
    Two flannel shirts they've forgotten, Kari!

KARI: Well, so they have!

ÅSE:                     What a piece of luck!
    We can surely keep *one* of them –
    no wait – I think we must keep them both;
    the one he's wearing's so thin and worn.

KARI: Lord, Mother Åse, you know that's a sin!

_____

1. One of Ibsen's own hobbies as a boy at Skien was casting metal buttons. While the craze lasted, any scrap of metal about the house was apt to reappear as a more-or-less useful button.

ÅSE: Maybe . . . but you know what the Parson says –
   that all our sins shall be forgiven.

★

*Outside a newly built hut in the forest, with reindeer horns over
the door. It is dusk, and there is deep snow.* PEER GYNT *is
standing outside the door, fixing a heavy wooden bolt.*

PEER GYNT [*laughing from time to time*]:
   There must be a bolt. I must bolt the door
   against trolls. Against men and women, too.
   There must be a bolt – a bolt that will hold
   against little goblins and all their spite.
      They come when it's dark, and they rattle and knock:
   'Open up for us, Peer, we're as nimble as thoughts!
      Under your bed you will hear us rustle –
   among the ashes you'll hear us scuffle –
   we'll fly in your chimney like dragons of fire.
      Ha, Peer, do you think that your nails and your
         planks
   can keep out the spiteful goblin-thoughts?'
         [SOLVEIG *comes over the snow on skis; she has a
         shawl over her head, and a bundle in her hand.*]
SOLVEIG: God bless your work! Don't send me away,
   I had your message, you must receive me.
PEER GYNT: Solveig! It can't be! It is! It is!
   And you're not afraid to come to me here?
SOLVEIG: You sent a message by little Helga –
   but messages came in the wind and the silence;
   your mother brought one in all that she told me,
   and messages swarmed in my dreams in the night.
   The nights that were empty, the days that were dreary
   brought me your message . . . and now I am here.

Down there, all the light had gone from my life;
I had neither the heart to laugh nor cry.
I could not know what thoughts you were thinking,
I only knew what I had to do.

PEER GYNT: But your father –?

SOLVEIG: Nowhere in God's wide earth
have I any now to call father or mother.
I have left them for ever.

PEER GYNT: Solveig, my dearest –
to come to me?

SOLVEIG: Yes, only to you.
You must be all to me – friend and consoler.
    [*In tears*]
The worst was leaving my little sister –
no, even worse was to part from my father –
and worst of all that I had to leave
the one who had borne me at her breast.
No, God forgive me, I found it worst
to part from all of them together!

PEER GYNT: You know the sentence they passed last
    spring?
They took both my farm and my heritage.

SOLVEIG: It was not for your goods nor your heritage
that I cut myself off from all that was dear.

PEER GYNT: You know the terms? If I go beyond
this wood, any man is free to take me.

SOLVEIG: Coming here on my skis, I asked the way;
they said: 'Where are you going?' I answered 'Home'.

PEER GYNT: Then I've finished with nails and planks and
    locks,
I shall need no bars against goblin-thoughts.
If you dare to go in and live with me here,
this hunter's hut will be holy ground.

Let me look at you, Solveig. . . . Not too near –
I will only look. . . . Oh, how pure you are!
Let me lift you. How slim and light you are –
I could carry you, Solveig, and never tire.
I shall not stain you – see, at arms' length
I shall hold you thus – so sweet and warm.
Who would have thought I could draw you here
the way that I've longed to, by night and by day.
See now, how I've been hacking and building. . . .
It shall all come down – it's too cramped and ugly –

SOLVEIG: Ugly or splendid, I'm happy here.
Here, in the buffeting wind, I can breathe;
down there it was airless, it hemmed me in.
It was partly for that that I came away;
but here, where the pine trees whisper above me –
such song, such silence – I am at home.

PEER GYNT: But are you certain? This is for ever.

SOLVEIG: There's no way back on the road that I've
come.

PEER GYNT: Then you are mine! Go in – then I'll see
you inside my house. I'll fetch wood for burning,
to cheer you warmly, and brightly light you;
you shall sit softly, and never be cold.

> [*He opens the door, and* SOLVEIG *goes in. He stands
> still for a moment, then leaps into the air, laughing
> aloud for happiness.*]

My royal princess! I have found her and won her –
and now a king's palace shall rise from the ground!

> [*He picks up his axe and starts to go. At the same
> moment, an* OLD-LOOKING WOMAN *in a torn
> green dress comes out of the wood. An* UGLY BOY,
> *with a flagon in his hand, limps after her, holding her
> skirt.*]

THE WOMAN: Good evening, Peer-of-the-Nimble-Foot!

PEER GYNT: Who are you?

THE WOMAN:     An old friend, Peer; I live quite close –
we are neighbours.

PEER GYNT:          Are we? That's news to me.

THE WOMAN: As *your* hut grew, mine rose beside it.

PEER GYNT [*starting to go*]:
I'm in a hurry –

THE WOMAN:     You always were, lad;
but I plodded behind, and I've caught up at last.

PEER GYNT:
You've made a mistake, woman.

THE WOMAN:                    Yes – long ago!
Back on the day when you promised so much.

PEER GYNT: I promised so much? What the devil is this?

THE WOMAN: You forget the night when you drank at
my father's;
you forget –

PEER GYNT:  I forget what I never knew!
What nonsense you're talking! Just when did we meet?

THE WOMAN: The last time we met was the first time we
met.
[*To the* BOY]
Your father's thirsty, boy, give him a drink.

PEER GYNT: His father?[1] You're drunk! Are you trying to
tell me –?

THE WOMAN: You can know a pig from the look of its
skin!

1. The story of the Ugly Boy and his flagon is another of the Gud-
brandsdal stories; but when Ibsen became apprenticed to an apothecary in
Grimstad, he turned in his loneliness to the one person in the house who
seemed friendly – a servant-girl ten years his senior. For the next fourteen
years he paid maintenance on their son.

Where are your eyes? Can't you see he's as lame
in his shanks as you are lame in your mind?

PEER GYNT:

Do you really pretend –

THE WOMAN: Are you wriggling out of it?

PEER GYNT: That lanky brat –

THE WOMAN: He's grown very quickly.

PEER GYNT: Why, you hag of a troll, do you dare to
pretend –?

THE WOMAN: I tell you, Peer Gynt, you're an ill-mannered
ox.

Am *I* to blame if I'm not as lovely
as I was when you tempted me, out on the hillside?
When the autumn came and my child was born,
I had only the devil to act as my midwife –
so can you wonder I'm ugly now?
But if you would see me as lovely as ever,
just show that woman in there the door!
Drive her out of your sight and out of your mind.
Do that, my love, and I'll shed this snout!

PEER GYNT:

Stay away from me, Troll-witch!

THE WOMAN: Just see if I do!

PEER GYNT: I'll break your head!

THE WOMAN: You try it – I dare you!

Aha, Peer Gynt, I can stand hard knocks!
I shall come here again every single day –
I shall peep through the door and watch you both.
When you sit with that woman beside the fire –
when you're loving, and wanting to play and embrace –
I shall sit beside you and ask for my share.
Yes, she and I will divide you between us.
Good-bye, my dear. Go and get married tomorrow!

PEER GYNT:
You nightmare from hell!

THE WOMAN:                 Oh, I was forgetting –
you must bring up the boy, you light-footed scamp!
Do you want to go to your father, you imp!

THE BOY [*spitting at him*]: Pah! you wait, and I'll take the
axe to you!

THE WOMAN [*kissing the child*]: There! What a head you've
got on your shoulders!
You'll be just like your father when once you grow up!

PEER GYNT [*stamping his foot*]:
I wish you were both as far away –

THE WOMAN:                 – as we are near you?

PEER GYNT [*clenching his fists*]:
And all this comes –

THE WOMAN:         Just from thoughts and desires!
You're unlucky, Peer!

PEER GYNT:         It's worse for her!
Solveig – my dearest, my purest treasure.

THE WOMAN: Ah yes, the innocent always suffer –
as the devil said when his mother thrashed him
simply because his father got drunk!

[*She goes off into the wood with the* BOY, *who throws
the flagon at* PEER GYNT.]

PEER GYNT [*after a long silence*]:
'Go round about,' said the Boyg. So I must.[1]
My royal palace has crashed to the ground!
A wall has grown round her – and I was so near;
now everything's ugly ... my joy has grown old.
Go round about, lad; there's no way now
that passes straight from you to her. . . .

1. It is already in Peer's nature to 'go round about', however much he
may attribute the idea to the Boyg.

That passes straight? Yes, there *still* might be. . . .
There's a text on repentance, if I remember –
but what? What was it? I have no Bible;
I've forgotten it all, and there's no one here
in this savage forest to set me right.

  Repentance? Why, it might take me years
before I won through! My life would be empty.
To destroy something lovely and holy and fair,
then patch it together from fragments and shreds. . . .
You might patch up a fiddle, but never a bell –
you must never trample the leaf that's to grow.

  But it *must* be a lie, what the Troll-witch told me!
All those ugly deeds have passed out of my sight. . . .
Yes, out of my sight, but not out of my mind.
Those stealthy thoughts would follow me in:
Ingrid – the three girls that leapt on the hillside –
will *they* come, too, with their jeers and threats,
begging, like her, to be taken and held –
to be lifted gently in outstretched arms? . . .
Round about, boy! If my arms were as long
as the fir tree's branches – the pine tree's trunk,
I still should be holding her much too near
to set her down stainless and pure again.

  I'll go round about – as well as I can –
whether it bring me loss or gain,
till such thoughts as these are forgotten for ever.

> [*He goes a pace or two towards the hut, but stops again.*]

  But to go in now! Shamefaced and ugly!
To speak, yet keep silent – confess yet conceal.

> [*Throwing his axe aside*]

This is All Saints' Eve. . . . To meet her like this –
just as I am – would be sacrilege.

SOLVEIG [*at the door*]:
  Are you coming?
PEER GYNT:        Round about . . .
SOLVEIG:                What?
PEER GYNT:                    You must wait;
  it's dark, and I have a load to carry.
SOLVEIG: Let me help. We will share the burden.
PEER GYNT: No, stay where you are. I shall carry it all.
SOLVEIG: Don't be too long.
PEER GYNT:            Be patient, my love.
  Long or short, you must wait.
SOLVEIG:            I will wait.
        [PEER GYNT *goes down the forest path.* SOLVEIG
        *remains standing at the open half-door.*]

*

*Åse's hut. It is evening; the room is lit by the wood fire that is
burning on the hearth. The cat is on a chair at the foot of the bed.
ÅSE is lying on the bed, plucking restlessly at the bedclothes.*

ÅSE: Oh God, is he never coming?
  The hours go so slowly by.
  I cannot send him a message
  though there's still so much to be said,
  and so little time is left me.
  So soon! Who would have believed it?
  If I could only be certain
  that I've not been too harsh with the boy. . . .
PEER GYNT [*coming in*]: Good evening.
ÅSE:                Oh, my dearest!
  God be praised, you've come at last.
  How did you dare to come, though?
  Your life is in danger here.

PEER GYNT: My life? How much does that matter?
  I only wanted to see you.
ÅSE: This proves that Kari was wrong, then;
  and now I can go in peace.
PEER GYNT: Go? Why, what's this you're saying?
  and where do you mean to go?
ÅSE: Ah, Peer, now it's almost over –
  I shall not have much longer to wait.
PEER GYNT [*turning away and pacing across the room*]:
  There now! I was running from sorrow;
  thinking here, at least, I'd be free!
  Are you cold? Are your hands or your feet cold?
ÅSE: Yes, Peer, it will soon be done.
  When you see my eyes cloud over,
  then you must close them gently . . .
  and afterwards make me a coffin,
  and, my dearest, be sure it's a fine one. . . .
  Oh no, I forgot –
PEER GYNT:           Hush! Time later
  to talk about things like that.
ÅSE: Yes, yes.
          [*Looking restlessly round the room*]
              You can see what a little
  they've left me. That's always their way.
PEER GYNT [*with a shudder*]:
  There you go!
          [*Harshly*]
              Yes, I know it was *my* fault –
  but what good does reminding me do?
ÅSE: No, no – it's that damnable drinking
  that brought our misfortunes upon us.
  You didn't know what you were doing,
  my dearest, because you were drunk.

And after your ride on the reindeer,
no wonder you weren't quite yourself. . . .

PEER GYNT: Yes, yes, but let us forget that –
leave the whole thing alone, it was nonsense;
let us put aside anything sad
till later – till some other day.

[*He sits on the edge of the bed.*]

Now mother, let's gossip together
about everything under the sun,
and forget about wrongs and misfortunes
and everything bitter and cruel.
Why look – if that's not your old cat there!
Just fancy him being alive still.

ÅSE: He's sometimes so naughty at night –
but *you* should know all about that!

PEER GYNT [*turning away*]:
Now what's all the news in the village?

ÅSE [*smiling*]: There's a girl in these parts, so they tell me,
who's longing to go to the mountains . . .

PEER GYNT [*hastily*]: Mads Moen – has *he* settled down
yet?

ÅSE: – and they say she refuses to heed
the tears of her father and mother.
You ought to go down and look in there –
perhaps you, Peer, would know what to say. . . .

PEER GYNT: And what has become of the blacksmith?

ÅSE: Don't mention that dirty smith!
Rather than that, shall I tell you
the name of the girl whom I said –?

PEER GYNT: Well now, let's gossip together
about everything under the sun,
and forget about wrongs and misfortunes
and everything bitter and cruel.

Are you thirsty? I'll fetch you some water.
How short that bed is! Have you room there?
Let me look – yes, I surely remember
that bed! It was mine as a boy!
D'you remember how sometimes at evening
you used to sit down at my bedside
and, pulling the coverlet tidy,
you'd sing me old ballads and songs.

ÅSE: Yes, remember the sleigh-rides we played at –
that was after your father had left us –
we called the blanket a sleigh-rug,
and the floor was an ice-bound fjord.

PEER GYNT: Ah yes, but the best of all, mother –
I wonder if you can remember –
was our team of beautiful horses!

ÅSE: How could I ever forget?
It was Kari's old cat that we borrowed –
we made her sit on a stool!

PEER GYNT: We travelled by high road and low road
to Soria Moria Castle,[1]
the castle that's east of the sun –
the castle that's west of the moon.
A stick that we found in the cupboard
you used as a whip for our sleigh.

ÅSE: I sat up in front as the driver –

PEER GYNT: Yes, yes, you'd keep letting the reins fall
and turning around as we travelled
to ask: was I feeling the cold?
God bless you, you ugly old darling,
what a loving old soul you were.

1. Said to be derived from the mythical Arabian Islands of the Blest beyond the Red Sea. It is mentioned by Asbjørnsen: 'East of the Sun and West of the Moon' is the title of one of his tales.

Why are you groaning?

ÅSE: My back hurts –
these bare boards are terribly hard.

PEER GYNT: Sit upright, and then I can hold you.
There! Is that easier now?

ÅSE: Oh, Peer, I do long to be gone!

PEER GYNT: Gone?

ÅSE: Yes, gone; that's the one thing I long for.

PEER GYNT: What nonsense! Now, pull up the blanket
and let me sit down on the bed.
There! Now we can spend all the evening
singing old ballads and songs.

ÅSE: No, will you bring me my prayerbook –
I'm troubled so much in my mind.

PEER GYNT: In Soria Moria Castle
the king and the prince will be feasting;
just rest in the sleigh on the cushions
while I drive you there over the moor.

ÅSE: But, Peer darling, am I invited?

PEER GYNT: Yes indeed, both of us have been asked.

> [*He throws a cord round the chair where the cat is
> lying, then, taking a stick in his hand, he sits at the
> foot of the bed.*]

Gee up! Come on, stir yourself, Blackie!
Mother, you're sure you're not cold?
Ah, Granë's[1] got into his stride,
and now you can feel that we're moving!

ÅSE: Peer, what is that I hear ringing?

PEER GYNT: The silver bells of our sleigh, mother.

ÅSE: Ah, but their clanging's so hollow!

---

1. Sigurd's charger in the Saga of the Volsungs. The word means 'grey',
so Peer is driving a two-horse sleigh, with the cat doubling the parts of
Granë and Blackie.

PEER GYNT: That's because of the fjord that we're
    crossing.

ÅSE: I'm afraid! What's that roaring I hear –
that sighing so strange and wild?

PEER GYNT: It's the murmur of pine-forests, mother,
as we're crossing the moor. Just lie still.

ÅSE: Lights flicker and flash in the distance . . .
where are they shining from?

PEER GYNT: From the windows and doors of the castle –
there . . . can you hear the dancing?

ÅSE: Yes . . .

PEER GYNT: There at the gate stands St Peter,
he's bidding you come inside.

ÅSE: Is he welcoming me?

PEER GYNT:                   Yes, with honour.
He'll pour you their sweetest wine.

ÅSE: Wine? And will there be cakes, Peer?

PEER GYNT: Of course – on a loaded dish;
and there is the Provost's wife
bringing you coffee and fruit.

ÅSE: Dear Lord – shall I really meet her?[1]

PEER GYNT: For as long and as much as you like.

ÅSE: Oh, Peer, it's a wonderful banquet
you're bringing your old mother to!

PEER GYNT [*cracking his whip*]:
    Gee up! Step out lively there, Blackie!

ÅSE: Dear Peer, are you on the right road?

PEER GYNT [*cracking the whip again*]:
It's an easy road now.

---

1. Since the Provost, and presumably his wife, were frequent guests at
Jon Gynt's house in his heyday, it seems strange that Åse should be so im-
pressed. But originally Ibsen wrote 'The Virgin Mary'; when he revised
it he left this line unchanged.

ÅSE:                    But the journey
  has left me so weak and so weary.
PEER GYNT: The castle is towering above us –
  now the journey will soon be over.
ÅSE: Then I'll just lie back with my eyes shut
  and trust to your skill, my son.
PEER GYNT: Gallop then, Granë my charger!
  The castle is crowded with guests
  all flocking to cheer at the gates:
  'Peer Gynt and his mother are here!'
  What's that you say, Mister St Peter?[1]
  My mother is not allowed in?
  I think you could search for a long time
  till you find such a worthy old woman.
  As to *me* – well, the less said the better –
  I can turn and go back at the gateway.
  Of course I'd be glad if you'd have me . . .
  but if not – well, I couldn't complain,
  for I've trumped up more terrible stories
  than the devil himself in a pulpit!
  I've called my old mother a hen, too,
  at the way that she cackled and clucked;
  but *you* must respect her and honour her,
  and make her feel really at home.
  You won't find they come any better
  from these parts nowadays.
  Aha! Here comes God the Father!
  St Peter, you'll catch it now!
        [*In a deep voice*]
  'Now don't play the Jack-in-Office –
  You're to let Mother Åse come in!'
        [*With a loud laugh, he turns to his mother.*]

  1. '*Herr Sankt Peder*' in the original.

There, you see, didn't I tell you?
He's singing another tune now!
    [*Uneasily*]
Why do your eyes start out so?
Have you gone out of your mind?
    [*He goes to the head of the bed.*]
Mother, don't lie there staring –
speak to me – Peer – your son.
    [*He feels her hands and forehead cautiously. Then,
    throwing the cord back over the chair, he says quietly*]
There, you can rest now, Granë,
we've reached the end of the journey.
    [*He bends over and closes her eyes.*]
Thank you for all that you gave me –[1]
for beatings and lullabies.
And now in return you must thank me. . . .
    [*Touching her lips with his cheek*]
There, that was the driver's fare.[2]
KARI [*coming in*]: Ah, it's you, Peer – her deepest longings
and prayers are answered now.
Dear Lord, how soundly she's sleeping. . . .
Or is she –?
PEER GYNT: Hush, she is dead.
    [KARI *weeps by the body.* PEER GYNT *paces the
    room for a long time, stopping at last by the bed.*]
PEER GYNT: See my mother decently buried.
I must try to get safely away.
KARI: Are you going far?

---

1. Literally 'for all your days'. In the next line, *barnebys* is a nursery word, and its nearest English equivalent would probably be 'bye-byes'. I have translated it rather freely as 'lullabies'.

2. Literally 'thanks for the ride' (*tak for skids*), which is what one would say when paying or tipping a driver.

PEER GYNT:         To the seacoast.

KARI: So far?

PEER GYNT: Yes, and farther still.

      [*He goes.*]

spaggptales

impetuous

caring, loving toward
mother - joking
exploiting, uncaring about women
except for one.

Wanted most of all
to be human and
free

Believed he could
be great

Never wanted to
committ himself to
something he could
not undo

# ACT FOUR

*A grove of palm-trees on the south-western coast of Morocco.
There is an awning and rush matting, and a meal is laid.
Farther back in the grove, hammocks are slung. Out to sea, a
steam yacht flying the Norwegian and American flags is lying.
There is a dinghy on the beach. It is nearly sunset.* PEER GYNT,
*now a handsome middle-aged man with gold-rimmed spectacles
hanging on his chest, and wearing smart travelling-clothes, is
acting as host. Mr* COTTON, *Monsieur* BALLON, *Herr* VON
EBERKOPF, *and Herr* TRUMPETERSTRÅLE *have just
finished their meal.*[1]

PEER GYNT: Drink up, my friends! If man was meant
   for happiness, he should be happy!
   It's written: 'What is past is past,
   and what's done's done.' What may I pour you?
TRUMPETERSTRÅLE:
   Friend Gynt, you make a splendid host!
PEER GYNT: I'll share the glory with my banker,
   my chef, my steward –

1. Mr Cotton is thus named in the rough draft, but Ibsen changed this
to 'Master Cotton' in the fair copy, and so it appears in the printed text.
*Eberkopf* is German for 'Boar's-head'; *Trumpeterstråle* (pronounced Troom-
p'et-er-straw-leh) is Swedish for 'Trumpetblast'. Ibsen never forgave the
Swedes for not coming to the rescue of Denmark in the Prusso-Danish war
of 1863–4, in spite of their continual obsession with their past military
glories under Charles XII.

   The meal that is laid is *middagsbord*, which is literally luncheon, but a line
or two later we find that it is nearly sunset. This is not a slip on Ibsen's part,
*middagsbord* is eaten at any hour of the afternoon till about six – the one
at which it is never eaten is *middag* (noon).

COTTON: Very well,[1]
then let us toast all four of you!

BALLON: Monsieur, you have a taste, a *ton*,
such as one seldom finds these days
among men when they live *en garçon* –
a *je ne sais quoi* –[2]

VON EBERKOPF: Yes, an Air
of spiritual Enlightenment
and Cosmopolitan-Judgement-Sharing – [3]
a through-the-cloudrift-noticed Glimpse
unfettered by restrictive Bias,
a Coinage of high Exegesis,
an *Ur-Natur* – yet an informed one –
united in Perfection's Peak.
Is that not what you meant, Monsieur?

BALLON: Er – possibly. It does not sound
quite so impressive, said in French.

VON EBERKOPF: *Ach* well,[4] that tongue is so restricted!
But should we seek the true beginnings
of this phenomenon –

PEER GYNT: The answer
is simply that I've never married!
Yes, gentlemen, the thing's as simple

---

1. Ibsen uses the English words. At first he spelt it 'Werry well', but this is hardly an American usage, and in the third edition he corrected it.

2. Although the other French and German words in this scene were used by Ibsen in the original, he did not write *je ne sais quoi* – perhaps because of the difficulty of finding a rhyme for *quoi*. But what better translation of *jeg ved ej hvad* (I know not what) could there be in the mouth of a Frenchman?

3. Satirizing the German addiction to massive compound abstractions, Ibsen coins a magnificent twenty-eight-letter word that takes up the whole line except for an *og* ('and').

4. In the original. it is an uneasy marriage between the Norwegian *ej hvad* and the German *ach wass*.

as this: what ought a man to be?
Well, my short answer is 'Himself' ...
guarding himself and his possessions,
a thing he cannot do when burdened
with someone else's weal and woe.

VON EBERKOPF:
  But this for-and-within-one's-self existence
  has, I daresay, entailed a struggle?
PEER GYNT: It has indeed – when I was younger;
  but always I came out the winner.
  On one occasion, though, I nearly
  got captured – much against my will!
  I was a brisk, good-looking fellow,
  and, as it chanced, the girl I fancied
  turned out to be of royal blood. ...
BALLON: Of *royal* –?
PEER GYNT [*airily*]: A collateral. ...
  As well you know –
TRUMPETERSTRÅLE [*thumping the table*]:
                              These noble Houses!
PEER GYNT [*with a shrug*]: 'Highnesses' who set such store
  on keeping their escutcheon free
  from any base plebeian blot!
COTTON: And so the whole thing came to nothing?
BALLON: The family opposed the match?
PEER GYNT: Far from it!
BALLON:                    Ah?
PEER GYNT:                      You understand,
  reasons arose which made it wiser
  that we should marry rather soon. ...
  But candidly, the whole affair
  from first to last was most unpleasant.
  Some things I'm scrupulous about –

I like to stand on my own feet . . .
so when the lady's father came
with such equivocal conditions
as that I change my name and status
and sacrifice my noble titles,
and others more unpalatable,
not to say unacceptable –
I gracefully withdrew myself,
refused the fellow's ultimatum,
and so renounced my bride-to-be.

[*Tapping the table and looking pious*]

Ah yes, there is a Fate that guides us,
and one in which we men can trust!
That's very comforting to know.

BALLON: Was that the end of the affair?

PEER GYNT: Oh no, for there were complications:
certain outsiders took a hand
and started quite a hue-and-cry. . . .
Her young relations were the worst –
I had to challenge seven of them,
an incident I'll not forget,
though I emerged victorious.
It led to bloodshed, yet that blood
confirmed my personal esteem –
corroborating what I said
just now, that there's a Fate that guides us.

VON EBERKOPF: You have a view of Life's con-
ditions
that puts you in the ranks of Thinkers.
A commonplace philosopher
sees every detail separately
and never grasps things as a whole,
but you see comprehensively.

You measure all things by one Norm;
you focus every Rule of Life,
till all shine forth, like rays, from one
bright sun of Life's Philosophy!
And yet you never went to college?
PEER GYNT: I am, as I remarked before,
self-taught in all particulars.
I never learned methodically,
though I have thought and pondered much,
and read a bit on every subject.
I started this in middle-age,
when, as you know, it's heavy work
ploughing a page from top to bottom,
to try to take in all at once.
History I have learned piecemeal –
I've not had time for more than that;
and since one needs, in times of trouble,
something that's solid to rely on,
I've learned religion, too – in snatches –
that way, I find, it slips in better.
One should not gorge oneself with reading,
but rather, choose what will be useful.
COTTON: That's sensible.
PEER GYNT [*lighting a cigar*]: And now, my friends,
picture what my career has been.
What was I when I first went westward?
A penniless lad with empty hands!
Believe me, it was sometimes hard –
I had to struggle to get food.
But life, my friends, is always sweet
and death is bitter, so they say!
Well . . . luck was on my side it happened,
and old Fate was benevolent.

I prospered; and since I was careful,
my fortunes went from good to better;
till ten years later I was called
the Croesus of the Charlestown traders!
My name was known from sea to sea,
I had good fortune with my ships –
COTTON: What did you deal in?
PEER GYNT:                    I carried mostly
Negro slaves to Carolina
and heathen images to China.
BALLON: *Fi donc!*
TRUMPETERSTRÅLE: How *could* you, Brother Gynt?[1]
PEER GYNT: You think my enterprise transgressed
the bounds of what's permissible?
Yes, I felt that myself – most keenly,
and in the end I came to hate it.
But once one's started, as you know,
it's hard to extricate oneself;
and with a huge concern like mine,
that gave employment to some thousands,
to close the firm down altogether
becomes particularly hard.
I've never cared to 'burn my boats'.
I grant you, on the other hand,
I've always had a great respect
for what are known as 'consequences',
and when I've overstepped the mark,
I've always felt a bit uneasy.
Besides, I wasn't getting younger –
I'd nearly reached the fifty mark –

1. Trumpeterstråle calls him *Farbroer*, which is literally 'Father's Brother',
i.e. 'uncle'.

already some grey hairs were showing;
and though my health was quite outstanding,
one painful thought occurred to me:
who knows how soon the hour may strike –
the Day of Reckoning arrive
when sheep and goats are separated?

What could I do? To end my trade
with China was impracticable.
I found the answer: I began
another line of business there:
while shipping idols every spring,
each autumn I sent missionaries
equipped with all such requisites
as Bibles, stockings, rum and rice.

COTTON: All at a profit?

PEER GYNT:                  Naturally!
It worked! They laboured tirelessly.
For every idol that was sold,
one coolie was in turn baptized –
the one trade cancelled out the other.
My mission field was never idle,
its time was spent in counteracting
the idols that I trafficked in.

COTTON: Yes, but the Negro merchandise –?

PEER GYNT: Ah, there my morals triumphed too.
I felt the trade was hardly suited
to someone of advancing years –
one never knows when one might die!
Also, there were the thousand pitfalls
the Abolitionists had laid,
besides the risk of privateers,
and perils from the wind and weather. . . .
These things together turned the scale;

I thought: 'Now Peter,[1] trim your sails!
See if you can't retrieve your errors.'
So I bought land in Alabama
and kept my latest load of flesh –
which was of first-class quality.
They flourished, they grew sleek and fat –
a thing which pleased both them and me.
Yes, without boasting, I can claim
that I was like a father to them –
a fact which brought me rich returns.
I built them schools, so that their morals
were unremittingly maintained
up to a certain general standard;
I saw to it the indicator
never once dropped below that mark.
And then I dropped the whole concern –
sold the plantation as it stood,
livestock and all – both hair and hide!
I issued, as a parting present,
free tots of grog[2] to great and small,
till men and women all had skinfuls!
To widows, I gave snuff as well.
That's why I hope – unless the text
'He that performs no ill, does good'
is nothing more than idle talk,
my peccadilloes are forgiven,
and, more than most men, I can claim
my good deeds cancel out my sins.

1. So, here and elsewhere, in the original.
   Ibsen does not specify the State as Alabama – he merely says 'in the South'.
2. So in the original. In his first draft, Ibsen gave the widows 'bibles – twenty-five of them'.

*rationalizes + justifies his*
*actions*

VON EBERKOPF [*touching glasses with him*]: How comfort-
     ing it is to find
  a scheme of life that works in practice –
  uninfluenced by theory,
  untouched by clamour from without.

PEER GYNT [*who has been stealthily helping himself from the
     bottle during the foregoing*]:
  We Northerners know how to plan
  campaigns. The secret of success
  in life's affairs is very simple –
  it's this: to keep one's ears shut tightly
  against one serpent's deadly inroads.

COTTON: A serpent, my dear fellow? Which?

PEER GYNT: A little one that leads men on
  to do what is irrevocable!
     [*He drinks again.*]
  What the whole art of taking chances
  means – the art of having courage
  to do the things you want – is this:
  to keep your feet out of the cunning
  pitfalls that life prepares for us,
  and keep yourself thus free to *choose*.
  Remember that today's misfortunes
  are not the end – that life goes on;
  therefore be sure you've left behind you
  a bridge securing your retreat.
  That principle has been my standby
  and always influenced my actions –
  it's one that I inherited
  in childhood, from my native land.

BALLON: You are Norwegian?

PEER GYNT:               Yes, by birth;
  by inclination, though, I claim

citizenship of all the world.
For the good fortune I've enjoyed
I have to thank America.
My well-provided library
I owe to Germany's young thinkers.
From France, I get my taste in dress,
my manners and my nimble mind.
From England, an industrious turn –
besides an eye to the main chance.
The Jews have taught me how to wait.
From Italy I have acquired
a taste for *dolce far niente*.
And once, when up against the wall,
I somehow managed to scrape through
thanks to the help of Swedish steel.

TRUMPETERSTRÅLE [*raising his glass*]:
*Ja!* Swedish steel!

VON EBERKOPF:   Yes, first and foremost
we toast the man who wields a sword!

> [*They touch glasses and drink with* PEER GYNT.
> *The drink is beginning to go to his head.*]

COTTON: That, my dear sir, 's all very well,
but what *I'm* wondering about
is what you'll do with all your money.

PEER GYNT [*smiling*]: What will I do with it?

THE FOUR [*coming nearer*]:                    Yes, tell us.

PEER GYNT: Well, first of all, I mean to travel.
That's why I took you all on board
as fellow travellers, in Gibraltar.
I find I need a friendly chorus
to dance before my Calf of Gold.

VON EBERKOPF: That's witty!

COTTON:                     Yes, but no one hoists

his sails just for the love of sailing;
you have a goal, or I'm mistaken.
You want to be –?

PEER GYNT: An Emperor.

ALL FOUR: What?

PEER GYNT [*nodding*]: Emperor.

ALL: Of –?

PEER GYNT: – All the world!

BALLON: But how, my friend?

PEER GYNT: By force of money!
It's by no means a new idea,
it's been the core of all my dealings.
When young, I used to dream of roving
high as a cloud across the seas;
I soared with cloak and gilded blade –
and landed on all fours again!
But, friends, my goal remained the same.
Someone has said – or it is written
somewhere – I don't remember where,
that if you conquer all the world
yet lose your Self, all that you gain is
a wreath around your broken skull
– or words to that effect. That text
is by no means poetic nonsense.

VON EBERKOPF: But just what *is* the Gyntish Self?

PEER GYNT: That world inside my vaulted skull
which makes me *Me* and no one else . . .
just as a god can't be a devil.

TRUMPETERSTRÅLE: Ah, now I gather what your aim is.

BALLON: A great conception!

VON EBERKOPE: Most poetic!

PEER GYNT [*with rising excitement*]:
The Gyntish Self . . . it is a host

of appetites, desires, and wishes;
the Gyntish Self – it is a sea
of fancies, cravings, and demands;
in short – what stirs inside *my* breast
and makes me live my life as Me.
But as the Lord has need of clay
to make a world He can be God in,
so I, in turn, require some gold
to make myself an Emperor.

BALLON: But you have gold!

PEER GYNT:                    Ah, not enough!
Perhaps enough to last a day
or two as Emperor of some
such little place as Lippe-Detmold![1]
But I must be Myself *en bloc* –
must be the Gynt of all the earth;
I'll be Sir Gynt[2] from top to toe!

BALLON [*transported*]:
To own the world's most noted beauties!

VON EBERKOPF: – own all the vintage Rhenish wine![3]

TRUMPETERSTRÅLE:
– the Armoury of Charles the Twelfth!

COTTON: – but, best of all, an opening
for profitable trade –

PEER GYNT:          I've found
the way to gain them all! Which is
the reason why we've anchored here.
Tonight, we set sail for the North.

---

1. A tiny state of some 450 square miles in North Germany. At the time when Ibsen was writing *Peer Gynt*, it was still independent.
2. So in the original. Later in this scene, Ibsen calls him 'Sir Peter Gynt'.
3. Literally 'the hundred-year-old Johannisberger'.

The newspapers I have on board
have brought me some momentous news.[1]
[*He rises, and lifts his glass.*]
This shows that luck inevitably
helps only those who help themselves.

ALL FOUR: Well, tell us –!

PEER GYNT:　　　　　Greece is in revolt![2]

ALL FOUR [*springing to their feet*]:
What? Have the Greeks –?

PEER GYNT:　　　　　Yes, they have risen!

ALL FOUR: Hurrah!

PEER GYNT:　　　And Turkey is in trouble!
[*Emptying his glass*]

BALLON: To Greece! The path to Glory opens!
I'll aid them with my sword of France!

VON EBERKOPF: I with encouragement – from a distance.

COTTON: And so shall I – with armaments.

TRUMPETERSTRÅLE: At Bender I might find the famous
lost spur-buckles of Charles the Twelfth![3]

---

1. There is a difficulty here; was 'the reason why we've anchored here' to pick up the newspapers? But when Peer is stranded, he is terrified of being left alone in the desert. How does he get newspapers in so lonely a spot?

2. In the original, Ibsen has 'Hellas'. Greece revolted from Turkish rule in 1827, finally getting her freedom in 1838.

If, as the opening stage direction states, the play ends at 'about our own day' (1867), some forty years pass between Acts Four and Five, leaving Peer in his eighties at the end of the play.

3. Bender is a town in Bessarabia, usually spelt Bendery. After his defeat at Poltava in 1709, Charles XII collected his forces and remained encamped there until 1713. There is a story that when a Turkish messenger brought him the news that the Sultan had made a truce with Russia, Charles in his rage tore the man's clothes with his spurs. Be that as it may, the spurs are preserved in the Swedish Royal Museum, but their buckles are missing. What Ibsen actually wrote is literally 'In Bender I shall find the world-famous spur buckles,' but their fame is less world-wide than Herr Trumpeterstråle imagines, and they need explaining to English readers.

BALLON [*falling on* PEER GYNT's *neck*]:
    Forgive me, friend, if for a moment
    I misjudged you!
VON EBERKOPF:    I was a fool,
    I almost took you for a scoundrel!
COTTON: No, that's too strong . . . a simpleton.
TRUMPETERSTRÅLE [*trying to kiss him*]:
    I, Brother, for a specimen
    of the worst type of Yankee sharper.
    Forgive me.
VON EBERKOPF: We were all mistaken.
PEER GYNT: What do you mean?
VON EBERKOPF:                         Now at one glance
    we apprehend the Gyntish host
    of appetites, desires, and wishes –
BALLON [*with admiration*]: So *this* is the Essential Gynt!
VON EBERKOPF [*in a similar tone*]:
    A Gynt deserving of all honour.
PEER GYNT: But tell me –
BALLON:                    You don't understand?
PEER GYNT: No, gentlemen – hanged if I do!
BALLON: How's that? You'll surely set your course
    for Greece, with money and with ships –
PEER GYNT [*with a snort*]:
    No thanks! I'll help the stronger side!
    I'll lend my money to the Turks!
BALLON: Never!
VON EBERKOPF: Witty – but just a joke!
PEER GYNT [*is silent for a moment. Then he leans on a chair
            and assumes a serious expression*]:
    Gentlemen, listen . . . it is best
    we part, before the last remains
    of friendship blow away like smoke.

He who owns nothing can take chances.
He who possesses no more land
than can be covered by his shadow
is simply made for cannon-fodder.
But once a man has made his pile,
as I have, then his stake is greater.
*You* go to Greece; I'll land you there
and furnish you with weapons gratis.
The more you fan the flame of war,
the better it will suit my purpose.
Fight, then, for Freedom and for Right!
Charge on the Turks and give them hell –
and so with glory end your days
spiked on a Janissary's spear.
But please excuse *me*.
      [*Patting his pocket*]
                I have money,
and am Myself – Sir Peter Gynt!
      [*He puts up his sunshade, and goes into the grove
      where the hammocks are slung.*]

TRUMPETERSTRÅLE:
  The swine!

BALLON:    He has no sense of honour!

COTTON: Honour? Well, be that as it may;
  but what it could have meant to us
  in cash, if Greece had become free!

BALLON: I saw myself hailed as a victor
  by crowds of lovely Grecian maids!

TRUMPETERSTRÅLE: I saw those two heroic buckles
  safe once again in Swedish hands.

VON EBERKOPF: I saw my mighty Fatherland's
  *Kultur* advance by land and sea.

COTTON: The worst loss is material!

Hell![1] It's enough to make you weep!
I'd dreamed of owning Mount Olympus,
where, if reports are accurate,
there's native copper to be found
which would be well worth drilling for.
What's more, there's that Castalian Spring[2]
that people talk so much about;
its many falls would generate
a thousand horsepower at the least!

TRUMPETERSTRÅLE: I'm going still! My Swedish sword
outvalues all the Yankee gold!

COTTON: Maybe. But fighting in the ranks,
we should be swamped among the crowd –
what profit would there be in that?

BALLON: *Parbleu!* So near to fortune's summit –
then to be dashed down to the depths!

COTTON [*shaking his fist at the yacht*]:
*There's* the black cash-box that contains
the gold he sweated from his slaves!

VON EBERKOPF: An inspiration! Quick, come on!
His Empire is about to fall!
Hurrah!

BALLON: But what –?

VON EBERKOPF:          I'll seize his power!
The crew can easily be bribed.
On board! I commandeer the yacht!

COTTON: You *what*?

VON EBERKOPF:          I mean to grab it all!
          [*He goes to the dinghy.*]

1. Ibsen has 'Goddam' which is unlikely for an American. A few lines
later, I have made M. Ballon say *Parbleu*, though Ibsen uses a Norwegian
word.
2. The Castalian Spring is on Parnassus, not Olympus.

COTTON: My own best interests counsel me
to help you grab it.
[*He follows.*]
TRUMPETERSTRÅLE: What a rogue!
BALLON: A real rapscallion. But – *enfin* . . .
[*He follows the others.*]
TRUMPETERSTRÅLE: I think I'd better follow them –
but I protest to all the world . . .![1]
[*He follows.*]

\*

*Another part of the coast. It is moonlight, and there are drifting clouds. The yacht is making out to sea under full steam.* PEER GYNT *is running along the shore, sometimes pinching himself in the arm,[2] and sometimes staring out to sea.*

PEER GYNT: It's a nightmare! A mirage! I'll wake in a
minute!
She's steaming away just as fast as she can!
A mirage, that's all! I'm asleep, drunk or mad!
[*Wringing his hands*]
I surely can't possibly perish like this!
[*Tearing his hair*]
It's a dream! I insist that it *must* be a dream!
This is ghastly! Yet only too true, I'm afraid!
What treacherous friends! Oh, hear me, good Lord!

1. 'I protest to all the world' is a quotation from one of the numerous Notes sent out by the Swedish Foreign Minister, Count Manderström, when Prussia was invading Denmark. To Ibsen's great disgust, neither Sweden nor Norway would come to Denmark's aid.
2. To convince himself that he is awake – a nineteenth century affectation that went out with swooning, and may need explaining to younger readers today.

you're so wise and so righteous – do punish the brutes!

    *[Raising his arms]*

Lord, it's *me* – Peter Gynt! Oh, Lord, please pay attention –

unless you look after me, I shall be done for!

Make them lower the gig! Put the ship in reverse!

Stop the pirates! Make something go wrong with the
    works!

Think of *me* – and let other men's troubles go hang;

the world can look after itself for a little . . .

I'm damned if he's heard me. He's stone deaf – as usual.

That's a fine thing – a God who's run out of ideas!

    *[Beckoning upwards]*

Pst! Look, I've got rid of my Negro plantation;

I *did* send those missionaries into Asia!

Surely one good turn has earned me another?

Oh, help me to board her –

    *[A sheet of flame flashes skywards from the yacht,*
    *followed by thick smoke. A dull explosion is heard.*
    PEER GYNT *gives a cry and sinks down on the sand.*
    *When, eventually, the smoke clears, the ship has*
    *vanished.]*

PEER GYNT *[low-voiced and pale]*: A just retribution!

Sunk with all hands in the wink of an eye!

Eternal thanks for this stroke of luck!

    *[Moved]*

Luck? This was something far greater than that,

since I have been saved while those others have perished.

All thanks and praise that you heeded me

and, with all my faults, kept an eye on me.

    *[With a deep breath]*

What a wonderful feeling of safety and comfort

it gives one to know that one's specially cared for.

But where shall I find food and drink in this desert?
There can't be much here. Ah, but he'll understand,
so it isn't too desperate.

> [*Loudly and ingratiatingly*]
> > He won't allow
a poor little sparrow like me to go under;
I must humble myself – and leave matters to him.
If I just keep my chin up, the Lord will provide.

> [*He leaps up in terror.*]

Oh! Was that a lion that roared in the bullrushes?

> [*With chattering teeth*]

It couldn't have been.

> [*Pulling himself together*]
> > A lion, indeed!
Such beasts have a habit of keeping their distance –
they know it's not fitting to feed on their betters.
They know it instinctively, feeling – quite rightly –
that playing about with an elephant's dangerous.
  Be that as it may, I'll look round for a tree.
Over there I see palms and acacias waving;
if there's one I can climb, I'll be perfectly safe –
especially if I contrive to remember
a psalm or two.

> [*He scrambles up.*]
> > 'Morning is not like to evening.'
That text has been thoroughly weighed and examined....

> [*He settles himself comfortably.*]

How pleasant to feel so uplifted in spirit.
Thinking nobly is better than owning great riches.
Just rely on the Lord; he's aware of how much
of the cup of affliction I'm able to drink.
He takes quite a fatherly interest in me;

> [*Whispering, with a sigh, as he casts an eye out to sea*]

122

Economical, though? That he certainly isn't!

*

*It is night in a Moorish camp at the edge of the desert. Soldiers are resting round the camp fire.*

A SLAVE [*running in tearing his hair*]:
  The Emperor's[1] milk-white steed is stolen!
ANOTHER [*running in tearing his clothes*]:
  The Emperor's sacred robes are gone!
THE OVERSEER [*entering*]:
  A hundred strokes on the soles of the feet
  for you all, unless the thieves are captured!
      [*The soldiers spring to horse and gallop off in all directions.*]

*

*A grove of palms and acacias at dawn.* PEER GYNT *is up a tree, protecting himself with a broken-off branch from a swarm of apes.*

PEER GYNT: Ugh! What a most uncomfortable night!
      [*Laying about him*]
  What, are *you* back again? The damnable creatures!
  Is that fruit they're throwing? No! Something *quite* different!
  Really these apes are disgusting beasts!
  It's written 'Thou shalt watch and fight',
  But I can't go on, I'm far too tired.
      [*Impatiently, as the apes attack again*]

  1. Ibsen originally wrote 'Sheik'; in view of Peer's assertion that he means to become an Emperor, it might have saved some momentary confusion if Ibsen had not changed it.

I'll make them stop this filthy habit;
I'll try to catch one of the brutes –
hang him and skin him, then dress myself
as best I can, in his shaggy hide
so that they'll think I'm one of them.
What are we men? No more than dust;
and one *must* conform with local customs.
Another herd! They're everywhere!
Hop it, there! Shoo! They must be mad!
If only I could acquire a tail
or something to make me resemble the brutes –
        [*Looking up*]
What's that? Something moving overhead –
it's the old one – with paws chock-full of filth!
        [*He crouches apprehensively for a while without
        moving. The* APE *stirs, and* PEER GYNT *begins to
        beckon and coax him as if he were a dog.*]
Hello old fellow – are you up there?
You're a nice chap, eh? Just want talking to kindly.
*You* wouldn't throw things, would you now?
This is me! Hello! We're good friends, now aren't we?
Bow-wow! There, you see I can talk your language.
Why, old chap, you and I are very good pals –
I'll bring you some sugar tomorrow. . . . The brute!
The whole lot – all over me! Ugh, how disgusting!
Or perhaps it was food! It hasn't much flavour . . .
still, that's all a question of what you're accustomed to.
Now which philosopher was it who said
one must spit, and trust to force of habit.
Oh, here come the young ones!
        [*Fighting them off*]
                                It doesn't make sense
that Man, who's supposed to be Lord of Creation,

should have to endure – Oh murder! Help! Help!
The old one was foul, but the youngsters are worse!

★

*A rocky place overlooking the desert, with a cave, and a ravine
to one side. In the ravine are a* THIEF *and a* RECEIVER, *with
the Emperor's horse and robes. The horse, richly caparisoned, is
tethered to a stone. Horsemen appear in the far distance.*

THIEF: Spearmen's blades
   flashing, playing –
   See, see!
RECEIVER: I feel my noddle
   roll in the sand!
   Woe! Woe!
THIEF [*folding his arms over his chest*]: My father stole,
   his son must steal.[1]
RECEIVER: My father received,
   his son must receive.
THIEF: Accept thy lot
   and be thyself.
RECEIVER [*listening*]: Steps in the thicket!
   Fly! But where?
THIEF: The cave is deep
   and the Prophet strong.
[*They flee, leaving their booty. The horsemen disappear in the
distance.* PEER GYNT *appears, cutting a reed pipe.*]
PEER GYNT: Ah, what a glorious morning it is!

   1. This curious little scene was originally in prose, where it was between
a Horse Thief and a Stealer of Clothes (which explains why they appear
as 'Two Thieves' in Ibsen's list of characters). The point was more clearly
made that their calling was hereditary, rather than the result of mere chance.
When Ibsen put it into verse (in one of his rare departures from the four-
stressed line), he meant it to be set to music and sung.

The dung-beetle pushes his ball through the sand,
the snail comes creeping out of his shell.
Morning! It touches the world with gold![1]
How curious is the remarkable power
that Nature bestows on the light of day –
one feels so safe, one's courage increases,
one is ready, if need be, to fight with a bull!
How still it all is! Ah, these rural delights –
it's odd that I've always despised them till now!
To think men should shut themselves up in great cities
only to have themselves plagued by the mob.
Just look at the lizards – they bask in the sun
and scuttle about with no worries at all.
How well they obey the Creator's behest,
each fulfilling his special immutable role.
They are *themselves*, through thick and through thin –
*themselves*, as they were at his first order 'Be!'

> [*He puts his spectacles on his nose.*]

Here's a toad! Hidden deep in a block of sandstone –
completely immured – just his head peeping out
as if through a window. And there he sits watching
the world . . . and he is to himself – enough!

> [*Thoughtfully*]

'Enough . . .?' 'To himself . . .?' Now where does that
    come from?
Did I read it when young, in some so-called 'good
    book'?
Was it the prayerbook? Or Solomon's Proverbs?[2]

1. Literally 'Morning has gold in its mouth', a Norwegian saying which is a translation of the dog-Latin pun '*Aurora habet aurum in ore*'.

2. Ibsen has '*Salomons Ordbog*', which is literally 'Solomon's Dictionary'. In the first draft, he had *Ordsprog*, which is the normal word for the Book of Proverbs. Perhaps he meant the malapropism to underline Peer's general ignorance, but the joke is meaningless in English.

Dear me! How I find, as the years go by,
that my memory fails me for dates and places!
        [*He sits down in the shade.*]
It's cool here, I'll sit down and rest my feet.
There are ferns growing too. Have they edible roots?
        [*Tasting them*]
It's more suitable food for a beast than a man,
but it's written 'Thou shalt subdue thy nature',
and somewhere else, 'Pride shall be brought low',
and 'Who humbleth himself shall be exalted'.
        [*Troubled*]
'Exalted'? Yes, that's what will happen to me;
anything else is unthinkable.
The Creator will help me get out of this place,
and somehow contrive that I get a fresh start.
This is a test. My salvation will come
if only the Lord will grant me my strength.
        [*He shakes off these thoughts and, stretching himself,
        lights a cigar and looks out over the desert.*]
What an enormous and measureless waste!
There in the distance an ostrich is striding. . . .
What would you think the Almighty intended
in making this lifeless, monotonous desert?
This spot where all means of existence is lacking,
this burnt-out tract that can benefit no one,
this slice of the world for ever barren,
this corpse, that not since the world began
has rendered so much as thanks to its Maker?
What was it made for? Nature's a spendthrift!
Can that be the sea, shining there in the east?
No, that isn't possible – merely a mirage,
the sea's to the west, high above at my back,
dammed off from the desert by shelving dunes. . . .

[*A thought strikes him.*]
Dammed off? Then I might . . . The hills are low –
Dammed off . . . then a cutting – a simple canal,
and the water would pour in a life-giving flood
between the banks till it filled the desert!
It would quickly transform this whole burning grave
into a cool and rippling ocean.
What now are oases would stand out as islands;
northward, the slopes of Mount Atlas would burgeon
as green as the hills that run down to a fjord.
To the south, down the routes of the caravans,
white yachts would skim, as carefree as birds.
A life-giving breeze would refresh the air,
and dew would fall from the sky above.
Men would build themselves cities and towns,
and grass would grow round the swaying palms.
The land to the south of Sahara's limits
would change to a seaboard, with new-found trade;
there'd be steam for the mills of Timbuktoo,
and Bornu would be colonized.
Explorers' caravans would travel
from Habes[1] to the Upper Nile.
On a rich oasis set in my ocean
I'll settle men of our Nordic stock –
for dalesman's blood is almost royal,
and a drop of Arab will do the rest.
Round the sloping shore of a bay, I'll found
my capital, Peeropolis.
The world's played out – now it's the turn
of Gyntiana,[2] my youthful land!

1. Abyssinia.
2. When Ole Bull left the Bergen Theatre (where Ibsen worked as
'Resident Poet' from 1851 to 1857), he went to America where he tried to

[*Leaping up*]
Some money – and the thing is done –
a golden key to the ocean's door!
It's a Holy War waged against Death;
that grisly miser shall be forced
to free the gold that he has hoarded –
for every nation longs for freedom!
Like the ass in the Ark[1] I will send out a call
across the earth, then I will bring
the baptism of Freedom to those fair shores –
till now in bondage – that are to be!
I must press forwards! Am I to find
this money eastwards, or in the west?
My Kingdom – *half* my Kingdom for a horse!
[*The horse whinnies in the ravine.*]
A horse! And robes – and jewels – and weapons!
[*Going nearer*]
Impossible! Yet true! I know I've read
somewhere that faith can move a mountain,
but not that it can produce a horse!
Absurd! And yet the horse is there.
*Ab esse ad posse*, etcetera, etcetera. . . .
[*He puts on the robes and surveys himself.*]
Sir Peter! A Turk from top to toe!
One never knows what may become of one.
Come along, Granë, my noble steed.
[*He climbs into the saddle.*]
Gold stirrups, too, to hold my feet!

---

found a colony which he called 'Oleana'. It failed, and took all Bull's
savings with it.

1. From the riddle 'What ass could bray so loud that all men could hear
his voice?' 'The ass in the Ark.'

Great folk may be known by the mounts that they ride!
[*He gallops out into the desert.*]

*

*The tent of an Arab sheik, standing by itself in an oasis.* PEER
GYNT, *in his Eastern robes, is lolling on a cushion drinking
coffee and smoking a long pipe, while* ANITRA *and a bevy of
girls sing and dance for him.*

CHORUS OF GIRLS: The Prophet is come!
 The Prophet, the Lord, the All-Wise One!
 To us, to us, is he come,
 riding over the sandy sea.
 The Prophet, the Lord, the Infallible!
 To us, to us, is he come,
 sailing over the sandy sea.
  Sound the flute and the drum,
 the Prophet, the Prophet is come!
ANITRA: His charger is white as the milk
 that flows in the rivers of Paradise.
 Bend every knee; bow every head!
 His eyes are stars benignly gleaming;
 no child of earth would dare to meet
 the flashing rays those stars shine forth.
  Across the desert he came,
 with gold and pearls on his breast.
 Where he rode, came the light;
 as he passed, darkness fell.
 Behind him came drought and simoom.
 He, the Lordly One, came –
 across the desert he came –
 in the form of a mortal man.

The Kaaba,[1] the Kaaba stands empty,
he himself has proclaimed it.

CHORUS OF GIRLS: Sound the flute and the drum,
the Prophet, the Prophet is come.
        [*The girls dance to soft music.*]

PEER GYNT: I have read it in print, and the saying is true:
'In his native land no man is a prophet.'
And *this* life certainly suits me better
than the life I lived among Charlestown's traders.
There was something about it that struck me as false,
it was something essentially foreign – and shady,
I never felt really at home in the place,
or thought I was even the man for the job –
what on earth was I doing in that *galère*,[2]
rooting about among money-bags?
Thinking back, I can't understand it;
it happened like that, and that's all there is to it.

    To be one's Self on a basis of money
is exactly like building one's house on the sand.
True, the people will grovel, and kneel in the dirt,
before watches and rings and such trifles as that,
and they'll doff their hats to a coronet tie-pin,
but the ring and the pin are not really the man.
But a Prophet . . .! Ah, there the position's much clearer;
a man knows exactly on which foot he stands.
If he makes a success, the applause is for *him*,
and not for his pounds and his shillings and pence.[3]
He is what he is, and no nonsense about it,

1. The holy building at Mecca into which the sacred Black Stone is built. Anitra wrongly supposes it to be the grave of the Prophet.
2. Ibsen uses the Norwegian form *gallej*.
3. Though we might expect Peer to quote either American or Norwegian currency, he actually says *pundsterling og shilling*.

"in no way committed"

owing nothing to chance or to accident,
and independent of Patents or Deeds.
A Prophet! Yes, that's the position for me!
And yet I became one completely by chance –
simply by riding out over the desert
and chancing to meet with these children of nature.
Their Prophet had come, that was perfectly clear;
I certainly didn't intend to deceive them –
a Prophet's assent's not the same as a lie.
What's more, at a pinch, I can always retract –
I'm in no way committed; things might be much
    worse.
It's all, so to speak, just a private arrangement.
My horse is at hand, I can go as I came;
I'm the lord of the situation, in fact.

ANITRA [*approaching from the entrance to the tent*]:
My Prophet and Master!

PEER GYNT:            Well, what would my slave?

ANITRA: In front of the tent stand the sons of the Plain
craving a sight of thy countenance –

PEER GYNT:              Stop!
Tell them that they may form up at a distance;
say: from a distance I'll hear their petitions.
Add that I'll suffer no *man* to come in here.
  Men, my dear child, are a trivial lot,
in fact, one might well call them vicious and foul.
Anitra, you wouldn't believe how barefacedly
they've swindled – er, how they have sinned,[1] my child.
Well . . . enough of such things. Now dance for me,
    maidens;
your Prophet would banish such odious memories.

1. The resemblance between 'swindled' and 'sinned' is even closer in
Norwegian – *syndt* and *syndet*.

MAIDENS [*dancing*]: The Prophet is good; the Prophet is
    troubled
by the sins that the sons of the dust have committed.
The Prophet is gentle – all praise to his mildness –
he opens his Paradise even to sinners.

PEER GYNT [*his eyes following* ANITRA *as she dances*]:
Her feet are as swift as the sticks of the drummer . . .
ah, but she's really delicious, the baggage!
Her figure may be a bit over-developed –
not quite in accord with our standards of beauty.
But then, what is beauty? No more than a fashion,
a currency, changing with time and location;
and that over-development's just what appeals
to a man who has tasted the norm to the full.
A hide-bound man misses at least half the fun –
he finds a girl either too fat or too lean,
annoyingly young or revoltingly old;
the standard's insipid. . . .[1]
Her feet – well, they might be a little bit cleaner,
and so might her arms – especially *that* one.
But that, on the whole, isn't really a handicap –
in fact, I might call it a qualification. . . .
Anitra, come here!

ANITRA [*approaching*]: Thy slave is obedient.

PEER GYNT: Child, you attract me. Your Prophet is moved.
If you cannot believe me, I'll give you a proof:
I shall make you a houri in Paradise.

ANITRA: Impossible, Master.

PEER GYNT:               You think that I'm lying?
As true as I live, I'm in absolute earnest.

ANITRA: But I haven't a soul.

PEER GYNT:              Ah, then you can acquire one.

        1. This is a short line in the original.

ANITRA: But Master, how *can* I?

PEER GYNT:                          *I'*ll see to all that.
I shall take charge of your whole education.
No soul? I agree you're what might be called silly,
I've noticed that fact with a certain regret –
but pah! you could surely find room for a soul.
Just come over here, and I'll measure your head.
There's room; yes, there's room – I was certain there
      would be.
I admit it's unlikely you'll ever achieve
much depth. No, your soul would never be great;
but, damn it all, what does a thing like that matter?
You'll have quite sufficient to keep you in countenance.

ANITRA: The Prophet is kind, but –

PEER GYNT:                          You hesitate. Why?

ANITRA:
I would rather –

PEER GYNT:        Come on, you can speak without fear.

ANITRA: I'm not so concerned about having a soul,
won't you give me –?

PEER GYNT:              Well, what then?

ANITRA [*pointing to his turban*]:        That beautiful opal.

PEER GYNT [*captivated, as he hands her the jewel*]:
Anitra, you natural daughter of Eve,
you draw me like magic, since I am a man;
and, as a notable author once put it:
'*Das ewig weibliche ziehet uns an.*'[1]

*

1. Goethe in fact ends the line '. . . *zieht uns hinan*'. Archer thinks that
Ibsen is deliberately misquoting, so that Peer aptly says 'The Eternal
Feminine leads us on.' Other commentators claim, from the alterations and
erasures in Ibsen's manuscript, that he was unsure of Goethe's actual words.
However, for his Third Edition, Ibsen altered the spelling of *ziehet* to *zieht*;
if he had wanted to correct the quotation, he could have done so then.

*A moonlight night. In a grove of palm-trees outside* ANITRA's *tent,* PEER GYNT *is sitting under a tree with an Arab lute in his hands. His beard and hair are trimmed, and he looks considerably younger.*

PEER GYNT [*playing and singing*]:
  I locked the gate of Paradise
  and took away the key;
  while lovely women piped their eyes
  there where the ocean's margin lies,
  the winds bore me to sea.

  To the South – the South – my ship's course lay
  where salt sea-waves rise higher;
  where proud and fair the palm-trees sway
  like garlands round an ocean bay,
  I set my ship on fire.

  Then boarded I a desert ship –
  a ship that ran on legs,
  that foamed beneath my lashing whip.
  Catch me! I am a bird! I skip
  and twitter round my eggs!

  Anitra, thou art palm-tree wine,
  and well I know it's true.
  Cheese from Angora goats, though fine,
  is not by half so sweet to dine
  upon, my love, as you.
      [*He hangs the lute over his shoulder and comes
      nearer.*]
  Silence? Did my fair one listen –
  did she hear my little song?

Is she peeping through the curtain
innocent of veil – and so on?
Sh! That sounded like a cork
popping from a bottle's neck.
There again! And yet once more!
Was that a sigh of love? A song?
No, it was the sound of snoring . . .
sweet refrain – Anitra sleeps!
Nightingale, be quiet this instant
otherwise you'll pay for it
if you dare with cluck and gurgle. . . .
No. As the Good Book says: 'Sing on!'
Nightingales are music makers,
ah, and so am I myself;
he, like me, with music captures
tender gentle little hearts.
Night-time cool is made for song –
it's in singing we become
*ourselves*, Peer Gynt and nightingale;
and to know the maid is sleeping
is love's peak of ecstasy;
it's to raise a brimming goblet
to the lips, yet touch no drop!
But, upon my soul, she's coming!
This way's better, after all.

ANITRA [*from her tent*]: Lord, you called me in the dark-
    ness?
PEER GYNT: Yes, indeed, the Prophet called.
I was wakened by the ugly
racket of marauding cats.
ANITRA: Master, they were not marauding . . .
they were doing something worse.
PEER GYNT: What?

## ACT FOUR

ANITRA: Oh, please excuse me!

PEER GYNT: Answer!

ANITRA: Oh, I'm blushing!

PEER GYNT: Were they feeling
that emotion that possessed me
when I handed you my opal?

ANITRA [horrified]: Earth's Beloved! Who'd compare thee
with a dirty old tom-cat?

PEER GYNT: Child, there's not much difference –
looking on them just as lovers –
twixt a tom-cat and a prophet.

ANITRA: Lord and Master, from thy lips fall
honeyed jests!

PEER GYNT: My little friend,
like all girls, you judge us great men
merely by appearances.
Fundamentally, I'm sportive –
most of all when tête à tête –
though I'm forced by my position
and the weight of daily duties
to assume this sober front.
All my care and all my planning
on behalf of one and all
give me a prophetic curtness
– all, however, on the surface.
Balderdash! When we're together
I'm just Peer – that's who I am!
Let us, then, discard the Prophet;
then you're left with just – Myself!
        [He sits under a tree and draws her to him.]
Come, Anitra, let us dally
under this green palm-tree's fan.
I shall whisper, you will smile;

then we shall exchange our roles
and, as I sit gently smiling,
your young lips shall whisper love.

ANITRA [*lying at his feet*]: All thy words are sweet as music,
little though I understand.
Tell me, Master, can thy daughter
gain a soul by listening?

PEER GYNT: Later you will gain possession
of that light of life, a soul.
When the East, with rosy streamers,
tells in gold that dawn is here,
then, my girl, I shall have leisure
to begin your education;
But, in night's delicious silence,
even if I wished to do so,
I'd be foolish to endeavour
with some threadbare scraps of wisdom
to set up as pedagogue.
Souls, in fact, all things considered,
aren't of very great importance;
hearts are all that really matter.

ANITRA: Speak on, Master! When thou speakest
it is like the fire from opals.

PEER GYNT: Shrewdness in excess is folly.
That which buds as cowardice
later flowers as cruelty.
Truth, when it's exaggerated,
is but wisdom written backwards. . .
Yes, my child, I'd be a lying
dog, if I denied the world holds
people simply full of soul
yet without enlightenment!
Once I knew just such a fellow,

quite outstanding in his set,
yet this very man, mistaking
noise for reason, missed his goal.
See this desert, these oases?
If I merely wave my turban
I could make the world's great oceans
come and inundate it all.
I should be a perfect fool, though,
to go making seas and lands.
Do you know what life consists of?

ANITRA: Teach me.

PEER GYNT:      It's to be transported
dryshod down the stream of time,
still unchangeably one's Self.
Only in the prime of life, dear,
could I be the man I am.
Ageing eagles shed their feathers,
ageing beaux begin to stumble,
ageing beauties lose their teeth,
ageing men get wrinkled hands –
all of them get withered souls.
Youth, ah Youth . . . I mean to lord it
like a Sultan, strong and ardent,
not on Gyntiana's hillocks
not among its vines and palm-groves,
but among the verdant freshness
of a maiden's youthful thoughts.

So you realize, my sweet one,
why *you* are my gracious choice –
why it's *your* heart I've selected,
there to found – to coin a title –
my essential Caliphate.
I'll be master of your longings,

sovereign in my land of love!
You are to be mine entirely;
I will be the one who holds you
safe, like gold and precious stones.
Should we part, life would be empty
– *yours*, at any rate, please note!
All of you, each shred and fibre,
without will, or yea or nay,
shall be filled with none but me.
All your midnight-coloured tresses,
all of you that men call fair,
shall, like Babylon's rich gardens,
lure me to a Sultan's tryst. . . .

So you see, it's rather lucky
you should be so empty-headed;
those with souls are too self-centred
– too much wrapped up in *themselves*.
Yes, and while we're on the subject,
dammit, if you like, you may
have a ring to fit your ankle!
There! That's best for both of us:
you have *me*, why want a soul?
For the rest – the *status quo*!
        [ANITRA *snores*.]
What? Asleep? Did all I say go
in one ear and out the other?
Well, it proves how great my power is
when my torrent of endearments
wafts her far away in dreams.
        [*He rises, and puts more jewels in her lap.*]
Here are trinkets! Here are more!
Sleep, Anitra. Dream of Peer. . . .
Sleep! In slumber you have placed

a crown upon your Emperor's brow.
A personal triumph – that's the prize
Peer Gynt has won himself tonight!

\*

*The oasis is far in the background. Along a caravan route,* PEER GYNT *is riding through the desert on his white horse, with* ANITRA *before him on the saddle-bow.*

ANITRA: Stop it! I'll bite you!
PEER GYNT:                    You sweet little rogue!
ANITRA: What is it you want?
PEER GYNT:                    To play Falcon and Dove
  – to carry you off – to do scatterbrained things!
ANITRA:
  For shame! An old Prophet!
PEER GYNT                    What nonsense, you goose!
  The Prophet's not nearly as old as you think.
  Does *this* look to you like a sign of old age?
ANITRA:
  Stop! I want to go home!
PEER GYNT:                    You know you're just teasing!
  Home? To your stepfather? That would be fine!
  We two naughty birds who have flown from the cage
  must never come into his sight again.
  Besides, my dear child, it's not good for a man
  to stay for too long in a single place;
  he may gain some friends, but he loses prestige
  – especially if he's a Prophet or suchlike!
  He should show himself sparingly – brief as a song.
  It was certainly time for that visit to end . . .
  those sons of the desert are fickle at heart
  and both incense and prayers have been falling off lately.

*Vain*
*wants to keep youth*

ANITRA: Yes, but *are* you a prophet?

PEER GYNT:                    Why, I am your Emperor!
    [*Trying to kiss her*]
    Now now! Is my little bird[1] getting ideas?

ANITRA: Give me that ring that you've got on your
    finger.

PEER GYNT: Sweetest Anitra, they're trash – take them
    all!

ANITRA: Your words are like music, they echo so sweetly.

PEER GYNT: What rapture to find oneself loved so pro-
    foundly!
    I'll dismount! Then I'll walk by your horse as a slave
    would.
        [*Handing her the whip, he dismounts.*]
    See there, my rose! See, my tenderest blossom,
    how I will trudge through the sand at your side
    till sunstroke forbids me to go any more.
    I am young, my Anitra, please bear that in mind.
    You mustn't examine my actions too closely
    for follies and pranks are the earmarks of youth;
    and if only your intellect were a bit keener,
    then, little passion flower,[2] you would have noticed
    your lover is *full* of pranks – therefore he's young.

ANITRA: Oh yes, you are young. Have you any more
    rings?

PEER GYNT: I am young! Yes, take these! I can leap like a
    deer;
    if I had any vine leaves, I'd put on a wreath.
    Yes, my goodness I'm young. Look, I'm going to
    dance!

1. Literally 'my little woodpecker'.
2. Ibsen has 'oleander' – perhaps because the Norwegian word for it
(*Nerium*) is a convenient rhyme for *Kriterium* two lines earlier.

*abandon*

[*Dancing and singing*]
   I'm a happy little cock-bird,
   peck me – peck me, little hen!
   Allez-oop! Just see me dancing!
   Happy cock-bird once again.

ANITRA: You're sweating, my Prophet, I fear you might melt;
 that great bag at your belt – let me carry it for you.

PEER GYNT: So tender and thoughtful! Yes, carry the purse;
 without gold is a true lover's heart more contented.
   [*Dancing and singing again*]
   Young Peer Gynt is such a madcap
   he hardly knows which foot to stand on!
   Pah, says Peer, what does it matter?
   Young Peer Gynt has such abandon!

ANITRA: Oh joy, that the Prophet is treading a measure!

PEER GYNT: To blazes with prophecy! Now let's change clothes!
 Come on, take off yours.

ANITRA:         But your robe is too long,
 your belt is too wide and your stockings too tight.

PEER GYNT:
*Eh bien.*
   [*He kneels.*]
   Then inflict some sharp torment upon me!
 When a heart's full of love, it is pleasant to suffer.
 Listen, when once we get home to my castle –

ANITRA: Your Paradise? Have we much farther to ride?

PEER GYNT
A thousand miles . . .

ANITRA:       That's too far.

PEER GYNT:                  Only listen –
  you shall soon have that soul that I promised you would.
ANITRA: No, thank you; I'll get on all right with no soul.
  But you asked for some pain –
PEER GYNT:                Yes, damn it, I did;
  something piercing but short – lasting two or three days.
ANITRA: Anitra obeys you. So, Prophet – good-bye!
        [*She gives him a sharp rap over the knuckles, and
        races back across the desert at full speed.*]
PEER GYNT [*after standing for a long time as though thunder-
        struck*]:
  Well . . . who would have thought it . . .?

*

*The same place, an hour later.* PEER GYNT *is slowly and
reflectively taking off his Turkish robes, one by one. At last he
brings his little travelling hat from his pocket, and stands once
again in European clothes.*

PEER GYNT [*flinging his turban away as far as he can*]:
  There lies the Turk, and here stand I.
  A heathen existence is no good to me,
  I'm glad it was only put on with the clothes
  and not, as the saying goes, bred in the bone.
  Just what was I doing in that *galère*?
  It's certainly better to live as a Christian,
  rejecting the swaggering plumes of the peacock
  – founding your life upon law and morality
  – being *yourself* – ending up as a person
  who gets funeral orations, and wreaths on his coffin.
        [*He goes a few steps.*]
  That baggage! You know, she was only a hairsbreadth
  from making me thoroughly lose my head!

*rationalizes his mistake*

Although I'll be damned if[1] I understand
what on earth could have made me so silly about her.
Thank goodness it's over! A little bit later
I'd have come near to making a fool of myself.
I made a mistake. . . . It's a comfort to know
that my error arose from my false situation:
it wasn't that I was in error *myself*.
It was due to my living the life of a prophet
– a life with no savour of good honest toil –
that I was betrayed into . . . lapses of taste.
This being a prophet's a tiresome profession,
one's duties oblige one to live in a fog;
in acting the prophet, if once you behave
like a natural sensible person, you're lost!
A fact that I certainly proved to the hilt
by paying attention to *that* little goose. . . .
But nevertheless –

> [*He bursts out laughing.*]

                  What on earth was I up to?
Trying to put back the clock with my dancing;
as if swinging my hips could have held back the tide!
Kissing and sighing and playing the lute
– and getting well plucked in the end, like a rooster!
Prophetical frenzy – that's what you might call it!
Yes, plucked! To my shame, I've been thoroughly
    plucked!
Well, I've luckily still got a bit in reserve –
there's some in America, some in my pocket,
so I'm not quite reduced to the state of a beggar.
When all is said, *moderate* riches are best;
I'll not now be burdened with servants and horses,
I'll have no more trouble with coaches and luggage –

---

1. Literally 'I'll be a troll if . . .'.

*Choices*

in a word, I am master of that which is known
as the situation. . . . Which way shall I choose?
There seem to be many ways open before me.
It's the choice that distinguishes wise men from fools.
My financial career has become a closed chapter;
my amorous pranks I've cast off like a clout,
and I've no taste for scuttling back like a crab. . . .
'Forwards or backwards, it's just as far;
out or in, it's just as narrow' –
as I think it says in some clever book.
So . . . something new! Some enlightening quest!
Some goal that is worthy of money and pains.
Should I write my life, without any concealment –
a book that would serve as a guide and example?
Or wait – I have plenty of time on my hands,
suppose I turned into a wandering scientist,
laying bare the excesses of ages long past?
Yes indeed, that would suit me down to the ground;
I studied some legends when I was young,[1]
and I've added a lot to my knowledge since then.
I shall follow the path of the human race,
and float like a feather on History's tide,
re-living it all, as if in a dream.
I'll watch heroes do battle for honour and right
– from some safe point of vantage – an onlooker only;
see martyrs bleed and philosophers perish,
watch kingdoms founded and watch them crumble,
see great epochs growing from small beginnings –
in short, I shall skim off History's cream.
I must try to get hold of a copy of Becker[2]

1. As Ibsen himself did in the Gudbrandsdal.
2. Becker's *Weltgeschichte*, an account of the day-to-day life of Classical

and maintain, if I can, chronological order.
I grant that at present my scholarship's scanty,
and History's inner mechanics are subtle,
but pooh, very often the oddest beginnings
can lead to some really surprising results.
How inspiring it is to decide on a goal
then pursue it as firmly as marble or steel!
    [*With quiet emotion*]
To sever completely, from start to finish,
the ties that bind one to home and to friends;
to throw away one's entire store of riches;
to bid farewell to the pleasures of Love . . .
and all to solve the riddle of Truth!
    [*Wiping away a tear*]
*That* is the test of a man of Science.
It makes me happy beyond all measure
thus to have settled my destiny.
I need only stand firm through thick and through thin!
It's understandable if I swagger
and fancy myself: the man Peer Gynt –
also called Emperor of Mankind!
I'll become master of all the Past,
scorning to walk in the paths of the living.
The Present is not worth the sole of a shoe,
and the ways of mankind are deceitful and weak,
their intellects hidebound, their enterprise vain;
    [*Shrugging his shoulders*]
and women – well, they are the weaker sex!
    [*He goes.*]

       \*

---

Greece and Rome, had appeared in a Danish translation a year or two
earlier and was widely read in Norway.

*A summer day in the far North. A hut in the forest. Its open door has a strong wooden bolt, and there are reindeer horns above it. A handsome* WOMAN, *now middle-aged, sits and spins outside the hut in the sunshine.*

SOLVEIG[1] [*singing as she looks down the path*]:
   The winter and spring both may come, and pass by,
   And summer days may fade, and the year may die;
   But surely you will come back one day to me,
   And I shall still be waiting, as once I vowed to be.
        [*She beckons to her goats; then, resuming her spinning,
        she sings again*]
   God guard you, where e'er you may stray by sea or land,
   God comfort you, if now at His footstool you may stand;
   Here, until you come, I shall be waiting alone,
   And if you wait on high, I shall meet you there, my
      own.

*

*It is dawn in Egypt. The statue of Memnon stands in the sand.*
PEER GYNT *walks in, looking about him.*

PEER GYNT: This makes an excellent start to my pil-
      grimage;
   now, for a change, I've become an Egyptian,
   though one of essentially Gyntish design.
   Later, I'll make my way into Assyria. . . .
   If I started right back when the world was created
   I should only get myself thoroughly lost.
   In fact, I'll skirt round the whole Biblical story
   – I shall come on its traces in secular contexts,
   and to probe, as the saying goes, into its seams

   1. Ibsen calls her merely 'The Woman', just as he does with the Dovrë King's Daughter in the scene with the Ugly Boy. The translation is adapted to fit the Grieg setting.

is something beyond both my plan and my powers.
            [*He sits on a stone.*]
Now, I'll rest for a while, and wait doggedly here
till this statue produces his song to the dawn.
Next, after breakfast, I'll climb up the pyramid,
then, if there's time, I might look round inside it.
From there I'll go overland round the Red Sea
where perhaps I'll discover King Potiphar's grave.
Then I'll turn Asian. I'll seek out in Babylon
the fabulous Whore and renowned hanging gardens,
which are, so to speak, culture's earliest relics.
After that, I shall skip to the ruins of Troy;
and the sea-route from Troy surely takes me direct
across to the classical glories of Athens,
and there, on the actual spot, I'll inspect
every stone of the Pass where Leonidas fought.
I'll master the works of the better Philosophers,
find the cell in which Socrates laid down his life. . . .
No, now I remember . . . the country's at war!
Yes, Classical Greece must be put off until later.
            [*He looks at his watch.*]
It's really absurd what a long time the sun
is taking to rise . . . and my time is so precious.
Well now, after Troy – which was where I left off . . .
            [*He gets up to listen.*]
What's that very peculiar murmur I hear?
            [*The sun rises.*]
THE STATUE OF MEMNON [*singing*]:
            From the Demi-god's ashes rose songbirds
                    bringing back Youth.
                Zeus, the All-knowing one,
                shaped them for conflict.
                Oh, Owls of Wisdom,

Where are my songbirds sleeping?
You must die unless you fathom
   this, my song's riddle.[1]

PEER GYNT: I honestly do believe that the statue
   was singing. This must be Antiquity's Music![2]
The voice rose and fell in the stone. Yes, I heard it.
I'll just make a note to submit to the scholars.

   [*Writing in his notebook*]

'The statue sang. I could hear it distinctly,
though I failed to interpret the words of the song.
It was all a hallucination, of course.
Otherwise nothing worth noting today.'[3]

   [*He moves on.*]

\*

*The Great Sphinx, carved from solid rock, stands by the village
of Gizeh, with the spires and minarets of Cairo in the distance.*
PEER GYNT *enters. He examines the Sphinx minutely, some-
times through his spectacles and sometimes through his cupped
hand.*

1. Memnon was an Ethiopian who fought on the Trojan side and was
slain by Achilles. His mother, Eos, the Dawn, begged Zeus to confer some
honour on his corpse, so from the ashes of his pyre Zeus created a flock of
birds who flew three times round, then fought each other to the death and
fell on the pyre as a funeral sacrifice. The Owl of Wisdom is the badge of
the University of Norway, and Ibsen is said to be tilting at the professors
for being too much wrapped up in the past of Norway and too little con-
cerned with her present and future. The University had backed the Nor-
wegian Government in its refusal to intervene on the Danish side against
Prussia. Memnon refers to the fighting spirit that once rose from the ashes
of the past, and asks where it is sleeping.

2. '*Fortidsmusik*', a gibe at Wagner's *Zukunftsmusik* – 'The Future's
Music', which was being much discussed at the time.

3. Ibsen is making fun of Lieblins the Egyptologist, who had written a
dull and pedantic criticism of *Brand*.

PEER GYNT: Now where in the world . . .? I seem to
    remember
  meeting something that looked like this hideous
      object. . . .
  Yes, I've certainly met it. But where? North or South?
  Was it a person? And if so, who was it?
  That statue of Memnon, I realized afterwards,
  resembled the so-called Old Man of the Dovrë –
  the way that he sat there so starchy and stiff
  with his rump ensconced on the stump of a pillar . . .
  but this quite remarkably hybrid beast,
  this changeling, that's lion and woman at once,
  did I get it out of a fairy tale,
  or is it something I really remember?
  A fairy tale . . .? Ah, I've got it now!
  It was the Boyg whom I cracked on the noddle . . .
  or dreamed that I did, when I lay in a fever.
        [Going nearer]
  The self-same eyes and the self-same lips . . .
  not quite so sluggish . . . a little more crafty. . . .
  But in all that matters, the rest is the same.
  So that's it, Boyg – you look like a lion
  when seen in daylight and from behind!
  Do you still talk in riddles? Let's try you out:
        [Calling to the Sphinx]
  Hi, Boyg, who are you?
A VOICE [behind the Sphinx]: Ach, Sfinx, wer bist du?
PEER GYNT:
  What? An echo that answers in German? How odd!
THE VOICE: Wer bist du?
PEER GYNT:                Quite passable German, too.
  A new discovery – all my own.
        [He notes it in his book.]

'Echo in German – with *Berlinner* accent.'

    [BEGRIFFENFELDT *comes from behind the statue.*]

BEGRIFFENFELDT:

  A man!

PEER GYNT: So *that's* who was doing the talking!

    [*Adding a note*]

'Later arrived at a different conclusion.'

BEGRIFFENFELDT [*showing signs of great excitement*]:

  Excuse me, *mein Herr*, but – a most vital question:

  What is it that brings you to this place *today*?

PEER GYNT: To pay my respects to a friend of my
    youth.

BEGRIFFENFELDT:

  Who? The Sphinx?

PEER GYNT [*nodding*]: Yes, I knew him in days gone by.

BEGRIFFENFELDT: Splendid! And after last night's events,
    too!

  My head is throbbing as if it would burst.

  You know him, man? Answer then! Speak! Can you
    tell me

  what he is?

PEER GYNT: What he is? Yes, I certainly can:

  he is *Himself*.

BEGRIFFENFELDT [*with a bound*]: Ah! Life's riddle is
    solved!

  And all in a flash! You are really convinced

  that he is Himself?

PEER GYNT:        He said so, at any rate.

BEGRIFFENFELDT: Himself! Then the hour of Upheaval is
    here!

    [*He takes off his hat.*]

  Your name, *mein Herr*?

PEER GYNT:        I was christened Peer Gynt.

BEGRIFFENFELDT [*in hushed wonder*]:
  Peer Gynt! Allegorical! What I expected . . .
  Peer Gynt! Yes, that is to say: The Unknown!
  'He that should come', as the prophecy told me.

PEER GYNT:
  Oh really? And now you've come out here to meet –

BEGRIFFENFELDT: – Peer Gynt! Enigmatic! Profound and
      incisive!
  Every word in itself is a marvel of learning!
  What are you?

PEER GYNT [*modestly*]: I've always attempted to be
  Myself. The rest you can find from my passport.

BEGRIFFENFELDT: That word again – so enigmatic in
      essence!
        [*He seizes him by the wrist.*]
  To Cairo! Interpretation's Emperor is found!

PEER GYNT: Emperor?

BEGRIFFENFELDT:        Come!

PEER GYNT:                        Am I really known –?

BEGRIFFENFELDT [*dragging* PEER GYNT *after him*]:
  Interpretation's Emperor – based upon Self!

*

*A huge courtyard in Cairo surrounded by high walls, and
buildings with barred windows. There are iron cages. Three*
KEEPERS *are in the yard. A* FOURTH *enters.*

THE NEWCOMER: Tell me, Schaffmann, where's the
      Director?

A KEEPER: He drove out this morning before it was light!

THE FIRST KEEPER: I think something's happened to him
      that's upset him!
  Last night –

ANOTHER:     Sh, be quiet! Here he is at the gate.

> [BEGRIFFENFELDT *brings* PEER GYNT *in, locks the gate, and puts the key in his pocket.*]

PEER GYNT [*to himself*]: He's really a splendidly erudite man,

almost all that he says is right over my head.

> [*Looking round*]

So this is your Scientist's Club, is it?

BEGRIFFENFELDT:                    Yes,

here you'll find all of them; here is the Circle
of the Seventy Interpreters[1] – lock, stock, and barrel
– and it's just been increased by one hundred and three!

> [*Calling the* KEEPERS]

Mikkel! Schlingelberg! Schafmann! And Fuchs –
Into the cages with you, this instant!

THE KEEPERS: Us?

BEGRIFFENFELDT: Yes, who else? Get along with you!
Quickly!

When the world's in a whirl, then we must whirl with it.

> [*He shuts them in a cage.*]

The mighty Peer has arrived here this morning –
You can guess the rest, I'm saying no more.

> [*He locks the cage and throws the key into a well.*]

PEER GYNT: But, my dear Herr Doktor – dear Herr Direktor –

BEGRIFFENFELDT: Let's have no more titles! I was those things once, but –

---

1. The translators of the Septuagint. One hundred and three is presumably the number of inmates of the Asylum who, Begriffenfeldt imagines, have now been added to the great Interpreters.

In one of Wergeland's poems there is a mad editor called Blasenfeldt; Ibsen at first intended to call his Professor 'Frasenfeldt'.

*Mikkel* is the Norwegian and *Fuchs* the German for 'fox'; *Schlingel* is 'rascal' in German, and *Schaf* is 'sheep'.

## ACT FOUR

Can you keep a secret, Herr Peer? I *must* talk!

PEER GYNT [*with growing uneasiness*]:
   What is it?

BEGRIFFENFELDT: First, promise you'll not be alarmed.

PEER GYNT: Well, I'll try. . . .

BEGRIFFENFELDT [*leading him away into a corner and
      whispering*]:
                        It's that Absolute Reason
   dropped dead here last night at 11 p.m.

PEER GYNT: God help us!

BEGRIFFENFELDT:        Ah yes, it's the greatest calamity,
   and in my position, it's doubly unpleasant,
   for till that emergency, this institution
   was really a madhouse.

PEER GYNT:                  A madhouse? Good heavens!

BEGRIFFENFELDT: But no longer, of course.

PEER GYNT [*hushed, and pale with fear*]: Now I see how
      things stand:
   This fellow is mad – and nobody knows it!
         [*He moves away.*]

BEGRIFFENFELDT [*following*]: I hope most sincerely that
      you've understood?
   I said Reason was dead, that was not strictly accurate.
   He's beside himself – he has got out of his skin –
   just like my compatriot Münchhausen's fox.[1]

PEER GYNT: Excuse me a minute –

BEGRIFFENFELDT [*holding on to him*]: Well, more like an
      eel –
   not a bit like a fox. He was flung at the wall

---

1. Baron Münchhausen claimed to have put his hand down the fox's
throat till he grabbed its tail, then skinned it by turning it inside-out. In
another of his yarns, he fired a nail from his gun, and so nailed a fox to the
door.

with a nail through his eye.

PEER GYNT:                          I must find some way out!

BEGRIFFENFELDT:  Then a slit round his neck, and –
    whoops! Off with his skin!

PEER GYNT: He's mad! He's undoubtedly out of his senses!

BEGRIFFENFELDT:  Now it's perfectly clear, beyond all
        contradiction,
    that this 'Outside-oneself-ness' will have the effect
    of complete revolution by land and by sea.
    Therefore all persons formerly held to be mad,
    since last night at 11 p.m. have been normal
    according to Reason's most topical phase.
    And, if one considers the matter aright,
    it follows that, at the aforementioned hour,
    so-called intellectuals started to rave!

PEER GYNT: You were speaking of time, and my time is
        precious –

BEGRIFFENFELDT: You mentioned your time? Yes indeed,
        that reminds me:
        [*He opens a door and calls*]
    Come out! The long-promised time is proclaimed!
    Reason is dead – long live Peer Gynt!

PEER GYNT: No, no, my dear fellow –!
        [*One by one, the lunatics come out into the courtyard.*]

BEGRIFFENFELDT:                          Good morning! Appear!
    And greet the dawn of Emancipation!
    Your Emperor is come!

PEER GYNT:                          An Emperor?

BEGRIFFENFELDT:                                  Certainly.

PEER GYNT: But the honour's too great – I don't really
        deserve it.

BEGRIFFENFELDT: False modesty? And at a moment like
        this?

## ACT FOUR

No, no!

PEER GYNT: If you'd give me a chance to consider –
I feel quite dumbfounded – I'll never live up to it.

BEGRIFFENFELDT: What? A man who has fathomed the
Sphinx's enigma?
– a man who's Himself?

PEER GYNT:                Ah, but that's just the trouble,
I *am* myself – from beginning to end.
But, unless I'm mistaken, in here it's a question
of being one's Self *beside* one's self.

BEGRIFFENFELDT: Beside one's self? No, you're com-
pletely mistaken;
here man is himself to the uttermost limit –
himself, and nothing beside whatsoever.
As himself, he progresses full steam ahead;
he encloses himself in a barrel of self;
in self-fermentation he steeps himself,
hermetically sealed with the bung of self,
between staves that were seasoned in self's own spring.
No one sheds tears for another's sorrows,
no one considers another's ideas.
We're ourselves in thought, and word, and deed –
ourselves to the springboard's uttermost edge . . .
so if we're enthroning an Emperor here,
it's obvious you are the very man!

PEER GYNT: I wish to hell –

BEGRIFFENFELDT:            Now don't let it depress you;
almost everything strikes one as strange at the start.
'Oneself . . .' Just come here and I'll show you a sample –
I'm picking at random the first one that comes.

      *[To a gloomy figure]*

Ah, Huhu, good morning! Now, now, my good fellow –
still going around like the picture of misery?

157

HUHU[1]: Can I help it, when the People
   year by year die untranslated?
      [*To* PEER GYNT]
   You're a stranger, will you listen?
PEER GYNT [*with a bow*]: By all means.
HUHU:                      Then lend an ear:
   Like a garland, far to Eastwards,
   stands the coast of Malabar. . . .
   Portuguese and Hollanders
   spread their culture o'er the land.
   Also living there are pockets
   of the native Malabaris.
   All these peoples rule the country,
   and they've muddled up the language.
   But in prehistoric ages
   the orang-utan was ruler –
   lord and master of the forests,
   free to snarl and free to slaughter
   just as Nature's hand had shaped him.
   So he grinned, and so he pulled faces,
   so he screamed aloud, unhindered –
   he was master in his kingdom.
   Then the foreign yoke fell on him
   – spoiled the ancient forest-language.
   So four centuries of darkness[2]

---

   1. In the list of characters he is described as 'a Language Reformer from the Malabar Coast'. Ibsen is satirizing the cranks who were struggling to rid the Norwegian language of all Danish influence, and to return to the old Norse tongue.

   The sudden change of metre – especially to one made all too familiar to us by Longfellow – is disconcerting for the reader. A Scandinavian would know that the metre was that of the ancient sagas.

   2. Between 1400 and 1800 Norway was under Danish rule.

fell upon the Monkey people.
As you know, protracted darkness
makes a people grow up stunted;
those first wood-notes have been silenced,
till today there's no more growling.
If we would express our feelings,
it must be by using *language*!
This constraint applies to all men,
Portuguese and Malabaris,
Dutchmen and the half-caste people –
everybody suffers from it.
I have struggled to promote our
true primeval forest speech –
tried to resurrect its body,
championed man's right to shriek –
shrieked myself, and shown how needful
shrieking is in all our folk-songs.
No one notices my efforts.
Now perhaps you see my grievance.
Thank you for your kind attention,
I'd be grateful for suggestions.

PEER GYNT [*to himself*]: It is written 'When in Rome
  do the things the Romans do'.
      [*Aloud*]
Friend, if I remember rightly,
in Morocco there are thickets
where orang-utans in hundreds
live without a Bard or spokesman.
*Their* speech sounds like Malabari –
it would be a pleasing gesture
if, like certain other statesmen,
you'd consider emigrating
for the good of your own country.

HUHU: Thank you for your kind attention,[1]
I will do as you suggest.
   [*With an expansive gesture*]
The East repudiates its singer –
The West has its orang-utans!
   [*He goes.*]
BEGRIFFENFELDT: Well, *is* he himself? I certainly think so;
he's full of himself, and of nobody else.
He's himself in all that he shows of himself –
himself because he's beside himself.
Now, come over here and I'll show you another
who likewise returned to his senses last night.
   [*To a* FELLAH *with a mummy on his back*[2]]
Well, noble King Apis, and how are things going?
THE FELLAH [*to* PEER GYNT, *distractedly*]:
 *Am* I King Apis?
PEER GYNT [*getting behind the* DOCTOR]: I'm sorry to say
that I'm not really clear about what's going on,
but, to judge by the tone of your voice, I should say –
THE FELLAH:
 Now *you're* lying, too!
BEGRIFFENFELDT:   Perhaps if Your Highness
would say how things stand. . . .
THE FELLAH:     I certainly will.
   [*Turning to* PEER GYNT]
You see whom I have on my shoulders?
He once bore the name of King Apis,
though he's now what is known as a mummy,
and is therefore completely deceased.
 *He* it was built all the Pyramids,

---

1. Ibsen repeats his earlier line word for word.
2. This royal mummy is another allusion to the Swedish obsession with their past glories under their warrior king Charles XII.

the mighty Sphinx also he fashioned,
and he fought, as the Doctor would put it,
both *rechts* and *links*[1] with the Turks.

    On this account, all Egypt
considered him immortal,
installing him in their temples
in the likeness of a bull.

    That *I* am this King Apis
is as clear to me as daylight,
and though *you* may not see it at present
you'll very quickly do so.

    The fact is, that King Apis, when hunting,
once got down from his horse for a moment
and withdrew himself to a corner
of the fields of my distant forebear.

    Now the ground that King Apis enriched thus,
has nourished me with its provisions
and, if any more proof is needed,
I possess invisible horns.

    It's a damnable shame, then, that no one
will ever acknowledge my greatness;
by birth I am Apis of Egypt,
though in other men's eyes, a mere fellah.

    Can you tell me just what I must do –
can you give me your honest advice
in this matter of how to become
the renowned, though deceased, King Apis?

PEER GYNT: Build pyramids, surely, Your Highness,
and a mighty Sphinx, too, you might fashion,

---

1. So in the original – Norwegian is short of words that will rhyme with 'Sphinx'.

    Although in the early acts Ibsen is careful to make his peasants speak very simply, this 'starving louse' of a Fellah has quite a literary turn of phrase.

and then fight, as the Doctor would put it,
both *rechts* and *links* with the Turks.
THE FELLAH: Well now, that's a fine thing to tell me!
A fellah! A louse and a starveling!
It takes all my time keeping my hovel
clear of the rats and the mice.
Quick, man, devise something better
to make me renowned and contented –
and also to make me resemble
King Apis who's here on my shoulders.
PEER GYNT: Why not hang yourself then, Your Highness?
And then, when laid deep in earth's bosom
and closely confined in your coffin,
be like one completely deceased.
THE FELLAH: I'll do it! My life for a halter!
To the gallows at once – bag and baggage!
At first I mayn't look so much like him,
but time will soon remedy that.
    [*He goes to make arrangements to hang himself.*]
BEGRIFFENFELDT: A personality, Herr Peer –
a man of method –
PEER GYNT:        Yes, I know –
but he'll really hang himself! God forgive us!
I don't feel well – my brain is whirling!
BEGRIFFENFELDT: A transitional stage, it won't last long.
PEER GYNT: Transition? To what? Excuse me, I'm off!
BEGRIFFENFELDT [*holding him*]:
Are you mad?
PEER GYNT:    Not yet. Mad? Heaven forbid!
    [*Uproar. The Political Minister* HUSSEIN[1] *forces his
    way through the crowd.*]
HUSSEIN: I'm informed that an Emperor came here today.

  1. Another gibe at the Swedish Foreign Minister, Count Manderström,

[*To* PEER GYNT]

Is it you?

PEER GYNT [*desperately*]: Well, they've made up their
minds that it is.

HUSSEIN: Good. Have you dispatches requiring an answer?

PEER GYNT [*tearing his hair*]:

All right – let them *all* come! The madder the better!

HUSSEIN [*with a deep bow*]: Would you do me the honour
of dipping me in?

I'm a pen!

PEER GYNT [*bowing still more deeply*]:

Then I am, quite clearly,

a rubbishy piece of imperial parchment.

HUSSEIN: My story, my Lord, in a few words, is this:
though they call me a sand-box,[1] in fact I'm a pen.

PEER GYNT: My story, Sir Pen, very briefly, is this:
I'm a sheet of paper that no one will write on.

HUSSEIN: People can't understand how I ought to be used –
they insist upon making me sprinkle sand!

PEER GYNT: I was the silver-clasped book of a lady . . .
mad or sane, it's the same printer's error!

HUSSEIN: Just think how frustrating it is for a quill
who has never a taste of the sharpening knife!

PEER GYNT [*leaping high in the air*]: Just imagine – to leap
like a buck from a crag,

down and down, never finding the ground underfoot!

HUSSEIN: A knife! I am blunt! make haste, someone, and
slit me –

the world will be ruined if nobody sharpens me!

who was inordinately proud of his style in the many Notes that he sent at
the time of the Prusso-Danish War.

1. In the ultra-conservative Swedish Court they still sprinkled sand
rather than use the new-fangled blotting-paper.

## PEER GYNT

PEER GYNT: What a shame for the world, which – like
  most home-made things –
  its Creator believed was especially good.

BEGRIFFENFELDT:
  Here's a knife.

HUSSEIN [*grabbing it*]: Ah, how I shall lick up the ink!
  What rapture to slit myself!
        [*He cuts his throat.*]

BEGRIFFENFELDT [*stepping aside*]: Kindly don't splash!

PEER GYNT [*in rising panic*]: Hold him!

HUSSEIN:                Yes, hold me – that's just the idea!
  Hold the pen – put some paper down on the desk. . . .
        [*He falls.*]
  I'm done for. The Postscript . . . pray do not forget:
  'He died as he lived – a pen guided by others.'[1]

PEER GYNT [*dizzily*]: What can I –? What am I? Hold
  tight! Great God –
  I'm whatever you wish: a Turk or a sinner –
  a hill-troll – but help me. My mind's giving way!
        [*He screams.*]
  I've forgotten your name in the heat of the moment,
  but help me – oh Thou who protecteth all madmen!
        [*He sinks down insensible.*]

BEGRIFFENFELDT [*taking a wreath of straw, he gives a bound
  and sits astride PEER GYNT*]:
  Ha! See how he triumphs in the mud –
  beside himself! A Coronation!
        [*He places the wreath on PEER GYNT's head, and
        shouts*]
  Long live . . . the Emperor of Self!

SCHAFMANN [*from the cage*]: *Es lebe hoch der grosse Peer!*

---

1. *En påholden pen* is one that an illiterate person would touch while
another person actually signed for him.

# ACT FIVE

*On board a ship in the North Sea off the Norwegian coast. It is sunset, and the weather is stormy.* PEER GYNT, *a vigorous old man with steel-grey hair and beard, is standing aft on the poop. He is dressed partly in seaman's clothes, with a pea-jacket and high seaboots. His clothes are rather worn and battered, while he himself is weatherbeaten and his expression is harder. The* CAPTAIN *is at the wheel with his* HELMSMAN; *the* CREW *is for'ard.*

PEER GYNT [*leaning his arms on the rail and looking towards the land*]:
There's the Hallingskarv[1] in his winter dress,
showing off, the old rogue, in the evening light.
And there's his brother the Jøkel, behind him,
with his ice-green mantle still on his back.
And the Folgefånn – how fine she looks,
like a maiden dressed in shining white.
Now you old boys, don't you try any tricks!
Stay in your places, you're just lumps of granite.
THE CAPTAIN [*shouting for'ard*]: Two men to the wheel!
And hoist the light!
PEER GYNT: The wind's rising.
THE CAPTAIN:                    Yes, it'll blow tonight.
PEER GYNT: Can we see the Rondë from out here at sea?

1. The Hallingskarv and the Jøkel are mountains and glaciers inland from Bergen. The ship must be approaching Trondhjem from the north-west for them to lie as Peer describes them. In fact, though, they could not all be seen at once. The pronunciations are *Hal*-lings-karrv, *Ye*(r)-kel, *Fol*-guh-fawnn', *Blaw*-hu(r), Gal-*he*(r)-pig-gun, *Haw*-taigh.

THE CAPTAIN: Oh no, it lies right behind the Fånn.

PEER GYNT: Or Blahø?

THE CAPTAIN:                    No, but from up in the rigging
on a clear day you might see Galdhøpiggen.

PEER GYNT: Where does the Hårteig lie?

THE CAPTAIN [*pointing*]:                    Right over there.

PEER GYNT: Ah yes.

THE CAPTAIN:        So you're not a stranger here?

PEER GYNT: I came this way when I sailed from home –
the dregs, as the proverb says, stay the longest.

            [*He spits and watches the shore.*]
In there, where the glens and the valleys show blue
and the narrower clefts are rugged and black,
below them, too, skirting the open fjord,
*those* are the places where people live!

            [*Looking at the* CAPTAIN]
Here in this country they build far apart.

THE CAPTAIN:                            Yes,
houses are few and far between.

PEER GYNT:                      Shall we
get in by daybreak?

THE CAPTAIN:        Yes, with luck;
unless the weather gets *too* bad tonight.

PEER GYNT: It's thickening out to westward.

THE CAPTAIN:                                Yes.

PEER GYNT: Oh – remind me, when we're settling up:
I'd like, as they say, to leave something behind
for the crew.

THE CAPTAIN: Ah, thank you.

PEER GYNT:                      It won't be much;
though I've made my pile, I've lost what I made.
Fortune and I are at loggerheads.
You know how much I've got with me on board –

that's all! The rest has gone to the devil!

THE CAPTAIN: That's more than enough to give you
some standing
with people at home.

PEER GYNT:        I have no people.
There's no one to wait for this rich old scarecrow. . . .
Well – at least I'll be spared any scenes on the quay!

THE CAPTAIN:
The storm's getting up.

PEER GYNT:      Yes. Now please don't forget
if some of your crew are really hard up
I won't be too stingy about the money.

THE CAPTAIN: That's kind of you. Most of them haven't
much,
and they've all got wives and children at home;
it's hard to get by on their pay alone,
so if they come home with a little bit more
it makes a reunion they'll remember.

PEER GYNT: What's that you say – they have children and
wives?
They are married?

THE CAPTAIN:     Married? Yes, every man-jack.
The one who's the worst off of all is the Cook;
back in his house there's sheer starvation.

PEER GYNT: Married? They've somebody waiting at
home?
Someone who's happy to welcome them, eh?

THE CAPTAIN:
Yes, poor folk are like that.

PEER GYNT:      And when they get back
in the evening –?

THE CAPTAIN:    Well, I should imagine their wives
have a special treat ready –

PEER GYNT: And a candle lighted?

THE CAPTAIN: Perhaps even two. There'll be something
to drink –

PEER GYNT: – and there they'll sit snugly – a fire on the
hearth,
their children around them, the room full of chatter,
with nobody able to finish a sentence
because they're so happy. . . .

THE CAPTAIN: That's how it'll be.
That's why you're so kind to be helping a bit
as you promised just now.

PEER GYNT: No, I'm damned if I do!
Do I look like a fool? Do you think I'd fork out
my money at random for other men's brats?
I've sweated too hard to earn what I've made. . . .
There's no one waiting for old Peer Gynt.

THE CAPTAIN: You must please yourself – your money's
your own.

PEER GYNT: You're right; it's mine and nobody else's.
We'll settle as soon as you drop the anchor:
my cabin and passage from Panama,
then a drink for the crew – and nothing else, Captain.
You can punch my jaw if I'll do more than that!

THE CAPTAIN: You'll get a receipt; I don't deal out
thrashings.
Now you'll have to excuse me, the storm is rising.

[*He goes across the deck. It has grown dark and the
lights have been lit in the cabin. The sea grows
rougher; there is mist and thick cloud.*]

PEER GYNT: To keep hordes of unruly children at home
who await your return with joy in their hearts –
to have someone's good wishes to take on your jour-
ney. . . .

But who's ever given a thought to me?
A candle lighted? Why, then, let it gutter!
I'll think of a way – I shall make them all drunk.
Not one of the devils shall go ashore sober!
They shall go home drunk to their children and wives,
they shall curse, and thump with their fists on the table
and frighten their dear ones out of their wits.
The wives will scream and run out of their houses
clutching their children. . . . I'll spoil their pleasure –

> [*The ship lurches sharply.* PEER GYNT *stumbles, and has difficulty in holding on.*]

Well, that was a proper battering!
The sea is working as if it were paid for it.
It's always the same in these northerly waters –
a cross-sea eternally headstrong and angry.

> [*He listens.*]

What was that cry?

THE WATCH [*for'ard*]: A wreck to leeward!
THE CAPTAIN [*giving orders, amidships*]:
Starboard your helm. Keep her close to the wind.
HELMSMAN: Are there men on the wreck?
THE WATCH:                    I could make out three.
PEER GYNT: Lower a boat!
THE CAPTAIN:            It would fill at once.

> [*He goes for'ard.*]

PEER GYNT: Fancy thinking of that!

> [*To some of the crew*]
>                    If you're men, you must save them!

If you *do* get wet, what the hell does it matter?
BO'SUN: It couldn't be done with a sea like this.
PEER GYNT: They're shouting again. Look, the wind is
    dropping.
Cook, will you risk it? Quick – I'll reward you.

COOK: Not if you gave me twenty pounds![1]

PEER GYNT: You dogs! You cowards! Have you for-
gotten
that these are men – with perhaps wives and children
waiting at home –

BO'SUN: Well, patience is virtuous!

THE CAPTAIN: Keep clear of those breakers!

HELMSMAN: The wreck has gone under.

PEER GYNT: Does that silence mean –?

BO'SUN: If it's true they were married,
the world is the richer by three new-made widows.

[*The storm increases.* PEER GYNT *goes aft across the
deck.*]

PEER GYNT: There's no trust left among men any longer,
nor the Christian faith that men speak and write of.
Their good deeds are few and their prayers are fewer;
they've no respect for the Powers above.
In a storm like tonight's, the Lord is prodigious;
those brutes ought to cringe, and reflect on the truth
that it's dangerous sport to take chances with elephants!
Yet there they were, openly flaunting His will!
*I* can't be blamed; when it comes to the point,
I can prove I was standing there, money in hand. . . .
Yet what good will it do? Still, the saying goes:
'Clear conscience makes the softest pillow.'
Yes – on land, perhaps, that may hold good,
but it's not worth a pinch of snuff on a ship
where honest men are hard to come by.
At sea you can never be Yourself . . .
you must go with the crowd – from the bridge to the
hold,
and if Judgement should fall on the Helmsman and Cook,

1. As before Ibsen uses *pundsterling.*

170

I expect I'd be lost with the rest of them.
Your personal merit just goes by the board –
You're no more than a sausage at slaughtering time.
   Where I've been wrong was in being too mild –
and look at the thanks that I've had for my trouble!
If I were younger, I might change my tactics
and try out a season of playing the boss.
There's time enough yet! It'll get round the parish
that Peer Gynt has come back from abroad – and on
      velvet!
By hook or by crook I shall get back the farm,
and I'll build the place up till it looks like a castle,
but I won't let anyone over the threshold,
they can stand in the doorway and twiddle their caps,
they can beg and entreat to their heart's content
but they won't get their hands on a farthing[1] of mine!
If *I*'ve had to suffer the buffets of fortune,
they'll very soon find I can hit out as well.

THE STRANGE PASSENGER[2] [*standing in the gloom beside*
      PEER GYNT *and giving him a friendly greeting*]:
Good evening.

PEER GYNT:   Good evening. . . . What? Who are
   you?

THE STRANGE PASSENGER: Your fellow passenger – at
   your service.

PEER GYNT: Oh . . .? I thought *I* was the only one.

THE STRANGE PASSENGER: A mistaken impression that's
   now corrected.

---

   1. *Skilling* – an obsolete coin worth less than a halfpenny.
   2. One of the things that angered Ibsen in Clemens Petersen's criticism
of the play was his assertion that this Strange Passenger represented 'Terror'.
'If I were on the scaffold,' wrote Ibsen to Bjørnson, 'and that explanation
would have saved my life, it would never have occurred to me. . . . I stuck
the scene in as a mere caprice.'

PEER GYNT: How odd, though, that I should never have
  seen you
  till now.

THE STRANGE PASSENGER: I never go out by day.

PEER GYNT: You're ill, perhaps? You're as white as a
  sheet.

THE STRANGE PASSENGER: No, thank you. In fact I'm
  uncommonly healthy.

PEER GYNT: The storm's getting worse.

THE STRANGE PASSENGER: Yes, thank goodness for that!

PEER GYNT: 'Thank goodness'?

THE STRANGE PASSENGER: The waves are as high as
  houses . . .
  it makes your mouth water just to think
  of all the wrecks that will founder tonight –
  of how many corpses will wash ashore. . . .

PEER GYNT: Heaven forbid!

THE STRANGE PASSENGER: Have you seen a man
  drown –
  or be hanged or strangled?

PEER GYNT:            You're out of your mind!

THE STRANGE PASSENGER: Corpses grin . . . but their
  laughter is very forced –
  and they've bitten their tongues through – most of them.

PEER GYNT: Keep away from me!

THE STRANGE PASSENGER:      One question first:
  if we, for example, should strike a reef
  and sink in the darkness –

PEER GYNT:           You think there's a risk . . .?[1]

---

1. Ibsen was particularly nervous about his health and safety. While he
was working on Act Three of *Peer Gynt*, there was a slight earthquake in
Ischia. Though it did not greatly disturb the inhabitants, Ibsen moved to
Sorrento the following day, where he finished the play. Even there he was

THE STRANGE PASSENGER: Oh, as far as *that* goes, how
     can I say?
  But suppose you were drowned and I was saved . . .?
PEER GYNT: Oh . . . nonsense –
THE STRANGE PASSENGER:     Well, it's possible, isn't it?
  And when a man stands with one foot in the grave
  he starts getting generous – goes in for charity –
PEER GYNT [*feeling in his pocket*]:
  Oh, it's money –?
THE STRANGE PASSENGER: No. But you might be so
     kind
  as to make me a gift of your excellent corpse?
PEER GYNT: You're going too far!
THE STRANGE PASSENGER: Just your corpse, you know!
  And all for the purpose of Science –
PEER GYNT:                              Clear off!
THE STRANGE PASSENGER: But think, my dear fellow –
     it's well worth your while.
  You'd be opened right up, and have daylight let in.
  – What I'm trying to find is the place where dreams
     lurk . . .
  I'd go carefully into each one of your crannies –
PEER GYNT: Get out!
THE STRANGE PASSENGER: But my dear sir, a water-
     logged corpse . . .!
PEER GYNT: You blasphemous creature! You'll bring on
     the storm!
  You must be quite mad – it's raining and blowing,
  the sea's out of hand, and we've very good reason
  for thinking we haven't much longer to live –
  and the way you behave is just asking for trouble!

---

disturbed by the news of an outbreak of typhoid in Naples, and he was
convinced that he and his wife had caught it.

THE STRANGE PASSENGER: You're not in the mood to
     discuss it just now,
  but time can effect really great transformations.
          [*With a friendly bow*]
  Well, if not before, we'll meet when you're drowning –
  perhaps *then* you'll be in a more tractable mood.
          [*He goes into the cabin.*]
PEER GYNT: What sinister fellows these scientists are
  with their Free-thinking ways.
          [*To the* BO'SUN, *as he goes by*]
                              A word, my friend:
  that passenger? Is he a lunatic?
BO'SUN: You're the only one here, so far as I know.
PEER GYNT: No one else? This is getting worse and
     worse!
          [*To a* SAILOR *who comes from the cabin*]
  Who was that went below?
SAILOR                         The ship's dog, sir.
          [*He goes.*]
THE WATCH [*shouting*]: Land hard ahead!
PEER GYNT:                         My trunks! My cash box!
  Get my things up on deck!
BO'SUN:                         We've got work of our own!
PEER GYNT: I was joking, Captain – pulling your leg!
  I'll help the Cook, you can take my word!
THE CAPTAIN: The jib has gone!
HELMSMAN:                         And there's the foresail!
BO'SUN [*crying out for'ard*]: Rocks ahead!
THE CAPTAIN:                         She's breaking up!
          [*Noise and confusion. The ship founders.*]

                         *

*Among the rocks and breakers off the coast. The ship sinks.*

*A dinghy with two men aboard can just be seen through the mist.
A wave breaks over it, and it fills and overturns. There is a
scream, followed by silence. After a while, a boat floating
bottom upwards comes into sight.* PEER GYNT *comes to the
surface beside it.*

PEER GYNT: Help! Send a lifeboat! Help! I'm drowning!
　　Save me, Lord – as the Good Book says!
　　　　[*He clings to the keel.*]
COOK [*coming up on the other side*]:
　　Oh please, Lord God, for my children's sake,
　　have mercy – let me get to land!
　　　　[*He clings to the keel.*]
PEER GYNT: Let go of that!
COOK: 　　　　　　　Let go yourself!
PEER GYNT: I'll smash your hands!
COOK: 　　　　　　　　Then I'll smash back!
PEER GYNT: I'll kick you and beat you into a jelly!
　　Let go your hold – she won't take two!
COOK: Let go!
PEER GYNT: 　No, *you* let go!
COOK: 　　　　　　　Not likely!
　　　　[*They fight. One of the* COOK's *hands is disabled, but
　　　　he clings fast with the other.*]
PEER GYNT: Let go that hand!
COOK: 　　　　　　　　Spare me, I beg you!
　　Remember that I have children at home!
PEER GYNT: I need my life much more than you –
　　I haven't any children yet.
COOK: Let go! You've had your life – I'm young.
PEER GYNT: Get off! Be quick! Drown – you're too
　　heavy!
COOK: Have mercy! Go, in heaven's name –

there's nobody to grieve for you.
> [*He slips off, with a scream.*]

I'm drowning!

PEER GYNT [*grabbing him*]: No, I've got your hair –
I'm holding you. Say 'Our Father . . .' Quick!

COOK: It's all gone dark – I can't remember. . . .

PEER GYNT: Leave out the unimportant bits.

COOK: 'Give us this day . . .'

PEER GYNT: Skip that bit, Cook,
you've had as much as you will need.

COOK: 'Give us this day . . .'!

PEER GYNT: What – that again?
It's plain that you were once a cook!
> [*His grip slackens.*]

COOK [*sinking*]: 'Give us this day our . . .'
> [*He sinks.*]

PEER GYNT: Amen, lad.
You were yourself right to the end!
> [*He swings himself up on the keel.*]

Well, where there's life, there's always hope.

THE STRANGE PASSENGER [*taking hold of the boat*]:
Good morning.

PEER GYNT: Huh?

THE STRANGE PASSENGER: I heard a voice –
how nice to meet you once again.
Well, I foretold this, didn't I?

PEER GYNT: Let go – there's hardly room for *one*!

THE STRANGE PASSENGER: Oh, I'm swimming – with
my left leg only – [1]
I'll float once I can get a grip
with just one finger in that chink.
Now, apropos your corpse –

---

1. Since the right leg might end in a hoof.

PEER GYNT: Shut up!

THE STRANGE PASSENGER:
But all the rest's completely lost –

PEER GYNT: Do hold your tongue!

THE STRANGE PASSENGER: Just as you like.
[*Pause.*]

PEER GYNT: Well?

THE STRANGE PASSENGER: I've shut up.

PEER GYNT: More devil's tricks!
What are you doing now?

THE STRANGE PASSENGER: I'm waiting.

PEER GYNT [*tearing his hair*]:
This'll drive me mad! *What* are you?

THE STRANGE PASSENGER [*nodding*]:
Friendly!

PEER GYNT: But what else? Tell me that!

THE STRANGE PASSENGER: What do you think? Who
else do you know
that looks like me?

PEER GYNT: I know that the devil –

THE STRANGE PASSENGER [*quietly*]: Is it his way to show a
lantern
on life's dark journey into fear?

PEER GYNT: Well! It turns out, when all is known,
that you're a messenger of light!

THE STRANGE PASSENGER: Friend, have you – even twice
a year –
honestly known what terror means?

PEER GYNT: One is afraid when danger threatens. . . .
Your words are slippery as eels!

THE STRANGE PASSENGER: Well, have you ever – even
*once* –
known that triumph that follows fear?

PEER GYNT [*watching him*]: If you've come to open a door
for me
you were stupid not to come before;
there's not much choice left to a man
when the sea's about to swallow him!

THE STRANGE PASSENGER: Then would your triumph
be more likely
if you were cosy by your fire?

PEER GYNT: Who knows. But how could you imagine
you'd move me with such empty talk?

THE STRANGE PASSENGER: Where *I* come from, a smile
is valued
as highly as a touch of pathos.

PEER GYNT: There is a time for everything;
and what is right for Publicans[1]
would, as the text says, damn a Bishop!

THE STRANGE PASSENGER: That multitude whose ashes
sleep
in funeral urns, don't *always* wear
the buskin of high tragedy![2]

PEER GYNT: Clear out, you monster! Go away!
I *won't* die! I shall reach the shore!

THE STRANGE PASSENGER: Oh well, as far as that's con-
cerned,
don't be alarmed – one doesn't die
right in the middle of Act Five!
[*He slips away.*]

PEER GYNT: Ah, so he's let it out at last:
he was a wretched Moralist!

*

1. Ibsen uses the word *tolder* – a Customs Officer. It is the word in the
Gospels that we translate as 'publican'.
2. Literally 'do not wear the cothurnus every day'.

*In a village in the high mountains, the peasants and their*
PRIEST *are holding a funeral in the churchyard. They are*
*singing the last verse of a psalm as* PEER GYNT *passes by on*
*the road.*

PEER GYNT [*at the gate*]: Here's somebody going the way
    of all flesh;
  thanks be to heaven it isn't me!
    [*He goes into the churchyard.*]
THE PRIEST [*speaking at the graveside*]:
  Now that the soul is summoned to its doom,[1]
  leaving the body here, an empty husk,
  let us exchange a word, dear Brethren,
  about the dead man's journey through this world.

    He was not rich, nor was he very clever;
  his voice was weak, his bearing was unmanly;
  he spoke his views with faltering diffidence,
  and hardly held the reins in his own house.
  He crept into the church as though he asked
  for leave to take his place like other men.

    As well you know, he came from Gudbrandsdal.
  He settled here when he was just a boy,
  and you'll remember how, up to the end,
  he kept his right hand always in his pocket.

    That right hand in his pocket was perhaps
  the only thing that stamped him on our minds –
  that, and this shamefaced reticence of his,
  this nervousness in everything he did.

    But though he chose to plod a silent road,
  and always seemed a stranger in our midst,
  all of you knew the thing he tried to hide –
  he had four fingers only on that hand.

1. The Priest's speech is in iambic pentameters – the only ones in the play.

I well remember, many years ago
during the War, one day I was at Lundë
when they were holding a recruiting board.
All men were talking of our country's hour
of danger – asking what the future held.

There, seated at the table, in between
the Bailiff and the Sergeant, was the Captain;
each boy in turn he carefully examined
and then enrolled and took him for a soldier.
The room was packed, and from the green, outside,
we heard the laughter of the waiting lads. . . .

A name was called; another lad stepped up,
pale as the snow along the glacier's edge.
They called him nearer. He approached the table.
He had his right hand bandaged with a cloth.
He gasped and swallowed, fumbling after words
but finding none, despite the Captain's orders.
Then, in conclusion, with his cheeks on fire,
his tongue now faltering, now pouring words,
he mumbled something of a scythe that slipped
and sliced his finger off. . . . A silence fell,
some exchanged glances, others pursed their lips,
their silent looks pelted the boy like stones;
and though his eyes were shut, he felt the blows.
At last the Captain rose, an old, grey man,
he spat, showed him the door, and said 'Get out!'

The boy went. Men fell back on either side
so that he ran the gauntlet through their ranks.
He reached the door, and then took to his heels.
Upwards he ran, up through the woods and moorland,
limping and staggering among the rocks
back to his home, high on the mountainside.

It was some six months later that he came here,

bringing his mother, child, and promised bride.[1]
He leased a patch of land up on the fells
among the wastelands bordering on Lomb.
As soon as it was possible, he married;
he built a house, and ploughed the stubborn ground
and prospered, as the patches of tilled land
bore witness in their pride of waving gold.
At church, he kept his right hand in his pocket,
but those nine fingers, at his farm, achieved
as much – and more – as ten of other men's. . . .
One spring, a torrent swept it all away!

Their lives were spared. Threadbare and penniless
he set to work to clear the land afresh,
and when the autumn came, smoke rose again
from a new farmstead in a sheltered place.
Sheltered? From flood, but not from avalanche –
for, two years later, it was overwhelmed.

But still disaster could not break his spirit;
he dug, he hoed, he carted, cleared the stones,
and, long before next winter's snowdrifts came,
he'd raised his humble homestead once again.

He had three sons – three fine strong boys. The school
was far away, and where the pathway ended
they had to climb through steep and narrow passes.
What did he do? The eldest had to climb
as best he could, but where the way was worst,
the father roped him to himself for safety;
he bore the others, one upon his back,
the other in his arms. So year by year
he laboured, and the boys grew up to manhood,
and he might well have looked for some reward. . . .

1. In the country districts there was no disgrace in postponing the actual
marriage ceremony till after a child was born.

In the New World, three prosperous gentlemen
have quite forgotten their Norwegian father,
and how he helped them on their way to school.

He was short-sighted; he could never see
beyond the narrow circle of things nearest.
Words that should rouse the heart like trumpet-calls,
seemed to him meaningless as tinkling bells;
high shining thoughts like Race and Fatherland
were always, to his vision, veiled in mist.

But he was humble – he was very humble;
and, surely as his cheeks had burned with shame,
he bore the brand of that Tribunal day,
and kept those fingers hidden in his pocket.
A breaker of his country's laws? Ah yes.
But there is something that outshines the Law,
just as the white tent of the Glittertind[1]
has clouds that shine in higher peaks above it.
He was no patriot – to Church and State
he was a barren tree. But on that upland slope
in the small circle where he saw his duty,
*there* he was great, because he was himself –
the metal he was forged from, there rang true.
His life was one long tune on muted strings. . . .
So – peace be with you, silent warrior
who fought a peasant's little war – and fell.

We shall not probe his heart – his inmost thoughts;
that is no task for us, but for his Maker.
But confidently I proclaim this hope:
he stands, uncrippled now, before his God.

> [*The congregation disperses and goes. Only* PEER
> GYNT *is left.*]

1. A mountain near the Jotunheim, famous for its gleaming white-
ness.

*Parson celebrates Self*

PEER GYNT[1]: Now *that*'s what I call a Christian spirit –
nothing to make one's mind uneasy.
The theme the Parson's discourse hinged on –
being inflexibly one's Self –
was, in the main, most edifying.
     [*He looks into the grave.*]
Was it he, perhaps, who hacked off his finger
the day I was felling trees in the forest?
Who knows . . .? If I didn't lean here on my stick
beside the grave of this kindred spirit,
I might think it was *I* who was lying asleep
hearing my praises sung in a dream. . . .
It's really an excellent Christian custom
to cast, as it were, a backward glance
benignly over the dear departed.
I should have no objection to getting *my* verdict
at the hands of this worthy parish priest.
Ah well, I've probably some time still
before I become the Sexton's guest;
and 'What's best is best' as the Scripture has it,
and likewise 'Sufficient unto the day . . .'
and also 'Take not thy funeral on credit.'
Ah yes, the Church is a fine consoler –
I've hardly considered the matter till now,
but I realize now how much good it can do
to be told – and with such authority –
that 'As ye sow, so shall ye reap',
that for everyone's sake you must be Yourself,
you must cherish your Self in all possible ways . . .
then if luck should give out, you still have the honour
of knowing you've always lived by your principles.

1. Another of Ibsen's violent changes of metre. Peer returns to the four-stressed line.

Now for home! The road may be narrow and steep
and fate may be mischievous right to the end,
but old Peer Gynt will go his own way
and still be his poor but virtuous self!
        [*He goes.*]

*

*A hillside with the dried-up bed of a stream beside which stands
a ruined mill.*[1] *The ground is rough, and the whole place is
desolate. Up the hill is a large farmhouse, and outside it an
auction is being held. There are many people present, and there
is a good deal of noise and drinking.* PEER GYNT *is sitting on a
rubbish heap by the mill.*

PEER GYNT: Backwards or forwards it's just as far,
    out or in, it's just as narrow.
    Time destroys, and the stream cuts through.
    'Go round,' said the Boyg . . . and so I must.
A MAN IN MOURNING[2]:
    Now there's only the rubbish left.
        [*He catches sight of* PEER GYNT.]
    You're a stranger here? Good day, my friend.
PEER GYNT: Well met. You seem busy here today –
    a christening? Or a wedding feast?
THE MAN IN MOURNING: I'd call it, rather, a homecoming
        party;
    the bride is sleeping with the worms.
PEER GYNT: And the worms are fighting for rags and
        tatters.

1. Though this might make us think that we had returned to the scene
of the opening of the play, this farm is in fact Hægstad.
2. This is Aslak the Smith. He has married Ingrid, and is now wearing
black for her funeral.

THE MAN IN MOURNING: This is the end of the song. It's over.

PEER GYNT: *All* songs end in the self-same way.
And they're old – I knew them when I was a boy.

A TWENTY-YEAR-OLD YOUTH [*with a casting ladle*]:
Look at the treasure that *I've* just bought –
Peer Gynt cast his silver buttons in this!

ANOTHER: What about me? A purse for a farthing![1]

A THIRD: Is that all? A pedlar's pack for fourpence!

PEER GYNT: Peer Gynt? Who was he?

THE MAN IN MOURNING: I just know he was
Death's brother-in-law . . . and Aslak the smith's.

A MAN IN GREY[2]: You're forgetting me. Are you mad or drunk?

THE MAN IN MOURNING: You're forgetting the store-house door at Hægstad.

THE MAN IN GREY: True – you were never particular!

THE MAN IN MOURNING: Let's hope she doesn't give Death the slip!

THE MAN IN GREY: Come, Brother-in-law . . . let's drink to our kinship!

1. The word Ibsen uses for 'purse' is *pengeskæppen* (literally 'penny-bushel'); it echoes the word *skæppen* that he used in the first scene where he called Peer's father 'Jon o' the Moneybags'. As in that speech, once again he rhymes it with *kramkarl-skræppen* (pedlar's pack). He is starting a series of allusions to Peer's early life. They are in chronological order, and Peer continues the list at his own 'auction' later in the scene.

As before, I have rendered *skilling* as 'farthing'; in the following line, Ibsen has *halvfemte* (literally 'half-five', or as we should say 'four-and-a-half'); 'fourpence' seemed a reasonable translation.

2. This is Mads Moen. In his first draft, Ibsen named both him and Aslak; it is hard to see why he should have made this rather puzzling alteration in his fair copy. It is this sort of thing that made Shaw, years later and in a different context, accuse Ibsen of being deliberately obscure. Ibsen replied, rather smugly: 'What I have written, I have written.' 'Yes,' retorted Shaw, 'and what you haven't written, you haven't written.'

THE MAN IN MOURNING: To hell with kinship – you're
  maudlin drunk!

THE MAN IN GREY: Oh nonsense – blood isn't as thin as
  all that!

  We must both feel a little akin to Peer Gynt.
    [*They go off together.*]

PEER GYNT: I'm meeting old friends!

A BOY[1] [*shouting after the* MAN IN MOURNING]: My poor
  dead mother

  will be after you, Aslak, if you go drinking!

PEER GYNT: The farming experts are wrong when they
  say

  that the deeper you plough the better it smells!

A YOUTH [*with a bear's skin*]: Here's the cat from the
  Dovrë![2] Its skin, at least!

  It drove out the trolls on Christmas Eve.

ANOTHER [*with a reindeer skull*]: Here's the marvellous
  reindeer that carried Peer Gynt

  along Gjendin ridge and over the cliff!

A THIRD [*with a hammer – calling to the* MAN IN MOURN-
  ING]: Hi, Aslak, is this the hammer you used

  that time when the Devil broke through your wall?

1. It has been suggested that this is the son of Peer and Ingrid, but more
than forty years have passed since Act One, and if there had been a child
it would now be grown up. The same applies to the suggestion that he
could be Mads Moen's son by 'pre-contract'. If he is Aslak's son, it is
strange that he should use his father's Christian name. It is possible that he
is merely a servant at the farm; the *matmor*, the mistress of the farm, would
be called 'mother' by all the servants.

2. An allusion to another of the Peer Gynt stories. One Christmas Eve
he went to free a particularly troll-infested farm. He took with him,
among other things, a tame white bear which he claimed was his cat, and
which frightened the trolls away. Years later, a troll asked the farmer if he
still had 'that big white pussy'. 'Yes,' said the farmer, 'she's got seven
kittens now!' 'Then you'll never see *us* again!' shouted the troll as he ran
away.

A FOURTH [*empty-handed*]: Mads Moen! Here's the In-
    visible Cloak
  Peer Gynt wore the night when he flew off with Ingrid!
PEER GYNT: Some brandy, lads! I'm feeling old –
  I must hold an auction of all my rubbish.
A YOUTH: What have *you* got to sell?
PEER GYNT:                    Well, there's a castle –
  it's strongly built, and it's up in the Rondë.
THE YOUTH: I'll bid a button!
PEER GYNT:               Make it a dram,
  it's a sin to bid any lower than that!
ANOTHER: He's a cheerful old boy!
      [*They all crowd round him.*]
PEER GYNT:             Then there's Granë my horse.
  Who'll bid?
ONE OF THE CROWD: Where is he?
PEER GYNT:               He's out in the West,
  near the sunset, my lads! That charger can fly
  as fast as – as fast as Peer Gynt could tell lies!
VOICES: What else have you got?
PEER GYNT:            There's gold and there's trash;
  they were bought at a loss, so I'll let them go cheap.
A YOUTH: Put them up.
PEER GYNT:          Here's a dream of a prayerbook
      with clasps . . .
  I'll let it go for a hook and an eye!
THE YOUTH: To hell with dreams!
PEER GYNT:             My Empire, then!
  I'll throw it you – there, you can scramble for it.
THE YOUTH: Does a crown go with it?
PEER GYNT:                Of finest straw!
  It will fit the first one who puts it on.
  Hi, there's more to come: A rotten egg!

A madman's grey hair! A Prophet's beard!
They shall go to whoever will show me the signpost
that says, on the hill-side: 'Here is your path.'

THE BAILIFF [who has come up]: I rather think, if you go on like this,
my man, that your path will lead you to jail.

PEER GYNT [hat in hand]:
Most likely. But tell me, who was Peer Gynt?

THE BAILIFF: What nonsense is –?

PEER GYNT: Please. It's a serious question.

THE BAILIFF: Well, he's said to have been a most shocking romancer.

PEER GYNT: Romancer?

THE BAILIFF: Yes – anything brave or fine,
he always claimed it was he who had done it.[1]
But excuse me, friend, there are things I must see to.
[He goes.]

PEER GYNT: And where is he now, this remarkable man?

AN ELDERLY MAN: He went overseas to foreign parts,
and came to grief, as you might have expected.
It's years ago now since he hanged himself.

PEER GYNT: Hanged himself? Well . . . I thought as much;
the late Peer Gynt was himself to the last.
[He bows.]
Good-bye – and thanks for a pleasant day!
[He goes a few paces, then stops again.]
You happy lads and charming women,
shall I tell you a story in return?

1. A man from Sel told Asbjørnsen, 'He was an odd fellow, that Peer Gynt – a great spinner of yarns. He told tales that I'm sure would have interested you. Even when they were adventures . . . from the olden days, he always claimed that he had taken part in them.'

SEVERAL VOICES: Yes, do you know any?

PEER GYNT:                      Of course – why not?

> [*He approaches. A curious expression comes over his face.*]

I was digging for gold in San Francisco;
the town was swarming with mountebanks –
one played the fiddle with his toes;
one, on his knees, danced a Spanish Halling;
a third, so I've heard, kept making rhymes
while they bored a hole right through his skull. . . .
To this tricksters' freak-show came the Devil,
to try his fortune like all the rest.
His claim was this: he was able to grunt
till you'd really have thought it a genuine pig.
He was quite unknown, but his manner was pleasing
so he soon had a full and expectant house.
He appeared in a cloak with an ample cape –
as the Germans say '*Man muss sich drapieren*' –
but nobody knew that beneath the cloak
he had somehow secreted an actual pig.
And so the Devil began his performance:
whenever he pinched it, the pig gave tongue . . .
it was all arranged as a kind of compendium
of the life of the pig – both domestic and wild,
to the final squeal at the slaughterer's knife;
after which the performer bowed low and retired.
The Critics discussed it and gave their opinions;
some praised the performance but others condemned it;
some found the tone of the voice was too thin,
some thought the squeal at the end too self-conscious,
but all were agreed on *one* point – that, *qua* grunt,
the sound of the pig was completely unnatural.
So that's what the Devil got for his folly

in overrating his audience.[1]

[*He bows and goes: an uncomfortable silence settles on the crowd.*]

\*

*Whitsun Eve, in a clearing deep in the forest: a little way off stands a hut with reindeer horns over the porch.* PEER GYNT *is crawling about in the undergrowth looking for wild onions.*

PEER GYNT: That's one stage finished, now what comes
        next?
    A man should try all things and then choose the best –
    which is what I've done . . . beginning with Caesar
    and now descending to Nebuchadnezzar.
    So I *did* have to touch on the Bible story!
    Now the greybeard comes back to his mother again –
    after all, as the text says, 'From earth hast thou come . . .'
    Well, the main thing in life is to fill up your belly;
    but to fill it with onions. . . . That isn't so good!
    I shall have to be cunning and set some snares.
    There's a stream full of water, I won't be thirsty,
    and I'll still rank as leader – among the wild creatures.
    And then when I die – as I probably shall,
    I can crawl in under a fallen tree
    and pull the leaves over me, just like a bear;
    and I'll scratch in big capitals on the bark:
    'Here lies Peer Gynt, a decent chap,
    Emperor over the animals here.'
    Emperor?
        [*He laughs to himself.*]
            You astrologer's dupe!

1. Peer, in his Auction scene, has tried to lay bare his innermost despair, and the crowd took it as a joke. Hence he tells them this fable.

You're no Emperor! Why, you're simply an onion –
and now, my good Peer, I'm going to peel you
and tears and entreaties won't help in the least.

[*Taking an onion, he strips it skin by skin.*]

There goes the battered outer layer –
*that's* the shipwrecked man on the dinghy's keel.
This layer's the passenger – scrawny and thin,
but still with a bit of a taste of Peer Gynt.
Next underneath comes the gold-mining Self –
the juice, if it ever *had* any, is gone.
This rough skin here, with the hardened patch
is the fur-trapping hunter from Hudson's Bay.[1]
The next one looks like a crown. No thanks!
We'll throw that away without a word.
Next the archaeologist, short but vigorous;
and here's the prophet, juicy and fresh –
it stinks of lies, as the saying goes,
and would bring the tears to an honest man's eyes.
This skin, curled and effeminate,
is the gentleman living his life of pleasure.
The next looks unhealthy and streaked with black –
black could mean either priests or niggers. . . .

[*He peels off several layers at once.*]

What an incredible number of layers!
Don't we get to the heart of it soon?

[*He pulls the whole onion to pieces.*]

No, I'm damned if we do. Right down to the centre
there's nothing but layers – smaller and smaller. . . .
Nature is witty!

---

1. Peer is working backwards over his life, so these gold-mining and
fur-trapping episodes happen in the forty-odd years that pass between the
opening of Act Five and the crowning with straw at the end of Act Four.
This is all we ever know of these years.

[*He throws the pieces away.*]
                 To hell with this brooding!
Once you start thinking, you trip yourself up.
Well, *I* at least can laugh at that danger
so long as I'm safely set down on all fours!
       [*Scratching his head*]
It's an odd situation, it certainly is!
Life, as he's called, plays with loaded dice,[1]
but grab at him, and he takes to his heels,
and you've caught something else – or nothing at all.
         [*He has come near to the hut. He catches sight of it and
         gives a start.*]
That hut on the hillside . . .? Well [*rubbing his eyes*] I'd
      have said
that I've seen that building somewhere before.
The reindeer horns on the porch . . . a mermaid
carved like a fish from the navel down . . .
Lies! There was never a mermaid . . .! But nails,
planks, and bars, to shut out goblin-thoughts. . . .
SOLVEIG [*singing in the hut*]:
         All is made ready for Whitsuntide.
         My dearest lad, though you're far away
            will you still bide?
         Is your burden great?
         Then pause and rest –
         still shall I wait
         as I professed.
PEER GYNT [*rising, quiet and deadly pale*]:
There's one who remembered, and one who forgot;
there's one who squandered, and one who saved.

1. Literally 'with a fox behind his ear', the Norwegian equivalent of
'with cards up his sleeve'. The next line carries on the fox metaphor, and
reads literally 'but if one grabs at him, Reynard leaps away'.

Oh, Destiny.... There's no turning back!
Oh, Sorrow! *Here* was my Empire set!
    [*He runs away down the forest path.*]

*

*A fir-tree heath at night. It has been ravaged by a forest fire,
and blackened tree-stumps stretch for miles. Patches of white
mist lie here and there among the stumps.* PEER GYNT *comes
running across the heath.*

PEER GYNT: Ashes and mist and wind-blown dust –
  here is enough for me to build with.
  Stench and rottenness inside –
  all a whited sepulchre....
  Tales and dreams and still-born knowledge
  form my pyramid's foundation;
  on them shall the work rise upwards
  with a scaffolding of lies.
  From the roof-top flaunt the motto:
  'Flee from truth and shun repentance.'
  Let the horns of Doom ring out with:
  '*Petrus Gyntus Caesar fecit!*'
    [*He laughs.*]
  What's this sound like children weeping –
  weeping that is half a song?
  Threadballs rolling where my feet tread –
    [*Kicking out at them*]
  Off with you – you block my path!
THE THREADBALLS[1] [*on the ground*]:
        We are thoughts,
        you should have formed us.

1. The dry husks of a plant which blow along the ground, rather like
the tumbleweed of America. They were popularly thought to be a mani-
festation of the trolls.

> Feet to run with,[1]
> you should have given us.

PEER GYNT [*going round about*[2]]:
> Life I gave to *one* – he proved
> a bungled, crooked-leggèd thing.

THE THREADBALLS:
> We *should* have soared skywards
> as challenging voices,
>> but here we must tumble
> like balls of grey yarn.

PEER GYNT [*stumbling*]: Threadball, you accursed lout,
> will you trip your father up?
>> [*He runs away.*]

WITHERED LEAVES [*flying before the wind*]:
> We are a watchword,
> you should have proclaimed us;
>> see how your idleness
> sadly has torn us.
> The worm has riddled us
> through every fibre;
> we never garlanded
> ripening fruit.

PEER GYNT: Your birth, however, was not in vain –
> lie still there, and you'll serve as compost!

A SIGHING IN THE AIR:
> We are songs,
> you should have sung us.
> A thousand times
> you have curbed and suppressed us.

---

1. Ibsen takes up the whole line with the word *pusselanker*; it is a nursery word, and its best translation would probably be 'tootsies', but that would hardly do here.

2. 'Going round about' are the Boyg's words.

In the depths of your heart
we have lain and waited. . . .
We were never called forth –
now we poison your voice.[1]

PEER GYNT: Poison yourselves, you foolish rhymes!
    What time had I for jingles and nonsense?
        [*He tries to escape another way.*]

DEWDROPS [*falling from the trees*]:
        We are tears
        that were never shed;
            we might have melted
        the ice-spears that wounded you.
        Now the barb festers
        in your rough breast,
        but the wound has closed over –
        our power is gone.

PEER GYNT: Thank you – I wept in that scrimmage on
        Rondë,
    and all that I got was a kick in the tail!

BROKEN STRAWS:
        We are deeds,
        you should have performed us;
            doubts that strangle
        have crippled and bent us.
        On Judgement Day
        we shall flock to voice
        our accusation;
        woe to you then.

PEER GYNT: An empty threat; you daren't accuse
    a man of what he *hasn't* done!

1. Literally 'Poison in your throat!' This is a strangely prophetic stanza,
since after *Peer Gynt* Ibsen was to turn away from writing verse, only to
find, years later, that he had completely lost the gift.

[*He hurries away.*]

ÅSE'S VOICE [*far away*]:

> You're a poor coachman!
> See, you've upset me
> here in the snow.
> Madly you've driven me,
> now you've bedraggled me.
> Peer, where's the Castle?
> The Devil's deluded you
> with the whip from the closet.

PEER GYNT: I must be off as best I can!
　If I'm to bear the Devil's sins,
　I'll very soon be underground –
　my own are quite enough for me.

> [*He runs away.*]

\*

*Another part of the moor.*

PEER GYNT:

> A sexton, a sexton! You lazy pack,
> 　open your bell-like mouths and sing!
> Tie round your hats your wreaths of black –
> 　I have plenty of dead for the burying!
> [*The* BUTTON MOULDER, *with his bag of tools
> and a great casting-ladle, comes along a side path.*]

THE BUTTON MOULDER: Gaffer, well met!

PEER GYNT: 　　　　　　　Good evening, friend.

THE BUTTON MOULDER:
　You seem in a hurry; where are you making for?

PEER GYNT: To a funeral feast.

THE BUTTON MOULDER: 　Ah. . . . My sight isn't good
　so excuse me, but surely your name must be Peer?

PEER GYNT: Peer Gynt's my name, yes.

THE BUTTON MOULDER: Now isn't that lucky!
Peer Gynt's just the man that I'm fetching tonight.

PEER GYNT: Oh, are you? What for?

THE BUTTON MOULDER: Well, as you can see,
I'm a moulder of buttons. You must go in my ladle.

PEER GYNT:
What becomes of me there?

THE BUTTON MOULDER: You'll be melted down.

PEER GYNT: Melted?

THE BUTTON MOULDER: You see? It's all empty and
clean.
Your grave is dug and your coffin ordered,
and worms shall feast in your skeleton.
And I have orders from the Master
to fetch your soul without delay.

PEER GYNT: You can't do that! I've had no warning. . . .

THE BUTTON MOULDER: That's always the way, both
with burials and births –
the day has been chosen secretly
and the principal guest gets no warning at all.

PEER GYNT: Yes, that's true. . . . But my head is spinning
round. . . .
Who are you?

THE BUTTON MOULDER: I told you – a button moulder.

PEER GYNT: Yes . . . a favourite child has many names.
Well, Peer, so this is the end of the road!
But you know, old chap, it's a shabby trick –
I'm sure I deserve to be treated better.
I'm not as bad as you seem to think;
I've done quite a lot of good in the world. . . .
The worst you can call me's a bit of a fool,
I'm certainly not an exceptional sinner.

THE BUTTON MOULDER: Ah, but, my friend, that's
  exactly the point;
in the strictest sense, you're no sinner at all.
That's why you escape the ordeal of the Pit
and go, with the rest, in the casting-ladle.

PEER GYNT: Whatever you call it – ladle or Pit –
bitter or mild, they're both of them beer!
Away with you, Satan!

THE BUTTON MOULDER: You can't be so dull
as to think that I limp on a cloven hoof.

PEER GYNT: On a cloven hoof or a fox's pad –
clear off! And kindly take care what you're doing!

THE BUTTON MOULDER: My friend, you're making a
  great mistake.
Now we're both in a hurry, and so, to save time,
let me explain to you just how things stand.
You are – and you've been the first to admit it –
not what they'd call an exceptional sinner
– not even a middling one –

PEER GYNT:                    *Now* you're beginning
to talk some sense –

THE BUTTON MOULDER: Wait just a moment –
but to call you virtuous goes too far.

PEER GYNT: No, I'd certainly never lay claim to
  *that*!

THE BUTTON MOULDER: Betwixt and between, then –
  half and half.
Nowadays one so seldom meets
a sinner on an imposing scale.
Sinning demands a strength of purpose,
there's a lot more to it than dabbling in dirt.

PEER GYNT: You're perfectly right in all that you say –
one must *rush* at it like the Berserkers of old.

THE BUTTON MOULDER: You, friend, on the other hand,
    took sinning lightly.
PEER GYNT: On the surface, friend – just a mere spatter of
    mud.
THE BUTTON MOULDER: So we're both agreed that the
    brimstone pit
 is not for you, who just dabbled in mire.
PEER GYNT: Then, friend, since that's so, can I go as I
    came?
THE BUTTON MOULDER: No, friend, since that's so,
    you'll be melted down.
PEER GYNT: What sort of tricks have you been up to
 here at home, while I've been abroad?
THE BUTTON MOULDER: It's a custom as old as the
    Serpent himself,
 its aim is to save wasting good raw material.
 Now, *you* know the trade – how it sometimes occurs
 that a casting turns out, as they say, with a flaw. . . .
 If a button occasionally hadn't a loop,
 what did you do with it?
PEER GYNT:              Threw it away.
THE BUTTON MOULDER: Ah, yes – Jon Gynt was known
    as a spendthrift
 so long as he'd anything left in his purse;
 but my Master, you know, is a thrifty man
 – which explains why he's also a wealthy one.
 He never throws out as completely hopeless
 what might turn out useful as raw material.
 Now *you* were designed as a shining button
 on the coat of the world . . . but your loop was missing,
 which is why you must go in the pile with the throw-
    outs
 to be what is known as 'reduced to an ingot'.

PEER GYNT: You can't be intending to melt me down
  with Tom, Dick and Harry,[1] to make something new?
THE BUTTON MOULDER: Yes indeed, that's exactly what
      I shall do,
  just as we've done with a great many others.
  That's what they do at the Mint,[2] with money
  when it's worn down smooth with too much use.
PEER GYNT: But that is disgustingly niggardly!
  Now look, my dear fellow, just let me go free.
  A loopless button, a farthing worn smooth –
  what are *they* to a man of your Master's standing?
THE BUTTON MOULDER: Ah, you see, the mere fact of
      your having a soul
  gives you a certain value as metal.
PEER GYNT: No! I say No! I shall fight tooth and nail –
  I'll put up with anything rather than that!
THE BUTTON MOULDER: Just *what*, for example? Now,
      listen to reason!
  You're not insubstantial enough for Heaven –
PEER GYNT: I'm humble – I'm not aiming nearly so high;
  but I don't mean to give up a jot of my Self.
  Let me be judged in the old-fashioned way –
  and sent down to the chap with the cloven hoof
  for a bit – for a century, if you're so harsh.
  You see, that's a thing that a man could put up with,
  for the torment would only be what he deserved,
  and it might even not be as bad as it's painted.
  After all, it's a change – as it says in the Book,
  and if, as the Fox said,[3] you wait long enough,

1. The Norwegian equivalent, 'Peer and Paul', might be confusing to us.
2. Literally 'at Kongsberg', the town in Southern Norway where the Royal Mint is.
3. A proverbial Norwegian saying; in full it is '. . . as the Fox said when they skinned him'.

the hour of deliverance comes, and it's over!
One hopes, in the meanwhile, for things to get better,
But this other idea – to be merged like a speck
within a completely irrelevant mass –
this ladle-affair – this cessation of Gynthood . . .
Why, it's an affront to my innermost soul!

THE BUTTON MOULDER: But Peer my dear fellow, it's so
    small a matter,
there's really no need to take on quite so badly.
Up till now, you have *never* been yourself,
so it's all the same if you die completely.

PEER GYNT: *I've never been* –? Oh, now don't make me
    laugh!
Do you mean that Peer Gynt has been somebody else?
No, no, Button Moulder, you've misjudged things badly.
If you could see into my innermost being
there you'd find Peer and nothing but Peer,
and never a vestige of anything else.

THE BUTTON MOULDER: But that isn't possible – here are
    my orders:
– look, I have it in writing: 'Collect Peer Gynt;
he has utterly failed in his purpose in life –
as defective goods, he must go in the ladle.'

PEER GYNT: What nonsense! It surely means somebody
    else.
Does it really say Peer? And not Rasmus? Or Jon?

THE BUTTON MOULDER: I melted down both of them
    ages ago.
Now, don't let's waste any more time; come along.

PEER GYNT: No, I'm damned if I do! A nice thing it
    would be
if tomorrow you found they meant somebody else!
You ought to be careful, you know, my good man;

remember it's you who're responsible. . . .

THE BUTTON MOULDER:

I have it in writing –

PEER GYNT: Well, just give me time –

THE BUTTON MOULDER:

What good will that do you?

PEER GYNT – and then I can prove
that I've been Myself for the whole of my life;
since it looks as if *that* is the heart of the matter.

THE BUTTON MOULDER:

Prove it? But how?

PEER GYNT: By witness and warranty.

THE BUTTON MOULDER:

I doubt if my Master will ever accept them.

PEER GYNT: But he must! Still, we'll cross that bridge
when we reach it.

Dear fellow – just *lend* me myself, on parole:
I'll be back again soon. Since we only live once,
we do tend to cling to the Self we were born with.
Well, do you agree?

THE BUTTON MOULDER: Oh, all right, I suppose so.
But remember – we'll meet at the next cross-roads.

[PEER GYNT *runs off.*]

*

*Much farther up the moor.*

PEER GYNT [*arriving at full speed*]: Time, as it says in the
Scriptures, is money.
If only I knew where the cross-roads are –
are they far away, or are they quite near?
The ground seems to burn me like red-hot iron!

A witness – a witness! Now where can I find one?
It's almost impossible here in the wilds.
A fine mess the world's in! We've come to the stage
when a man must find proof of his obvious rights!

> [*A crooked* OLD MAN, *with a staff in his hand and a
> sack on his back, hobbles up to* PEER.]

THE OLD MAN: Spare a copper, gentle sir, for a homeless
old man.[1]

PEER GYNT: I'm sorry, it so happens that I haven't any
change.

THE OLD MAN: It's Prince Peer – well fancy that, now!
So we two meet again!

PEER GYNT: Who are you?

THE OLD MAN:                    You've forgotten the old
greybeard in the Rondë?

PEER GYNT: But you *surely* can't be –

THE OLD MAN:                    Yes, I am – the Old
Man of the Dovrë.

PEER GYNT: The Old Man of the Dovrë? Are you really?
... The Old Man!

THE OLD MAN: Indeed I am. I've fallen upon very evil
days.

PEER GYNT: You're ruined?

THE OLD MAN:                    Yes, they've taken from me
everything I had;

and now I have to tramp the roads, as hungry as a wolf.

PEER GYNT: Hurrah – my luck's in! Witnesses like this
don't grow on trees!

THE OLD MAN: I notice that Your Highness has grown
grey since last we met.

---

1. With the entrance of the Old Man, Ibsen suddenly uses a longer line,
though still keeping to the regular four stresses. Later in the scene, the
shorter lines gradually reappear.

PEER GYNT: We all, dear pa-in-law, must bear the ravages
of time!

Well – let us set all personal transactions on one side,
and in particular, let's leave out family affairs.

What a very callow youth I was in those days. . . .

THE OLD MAN:                                 True, indeed;
but Your Highness was still young then, and youth will
have its fling.

It's lucky for Your Highness that you came to jilt your
bride.

By doing so, you've saved yourself disgrace and dis-
illusion;

for, since those days, the girl has gone completely to the
bad.

PEER GYNT: Well, well!

THE OLD MAN:          Yes, now she really is in rather
desperate straits –[1]

well, just imagine, she and Trond have run away together!

PEER GYNT

Which Trond?

THE OLD MAN: The one from Valfjeld.

PEER GYNT:                               Oh, from Val-
fjeld! Ha-ha-ha!

It was from him I took away three upland herd-girls
once.

THE OLD MAN: My grandson, now, has grown into a fine
upstanding lad;

all up and down the countryside he's fathered bouncing
babies –

PEER GYNT: Yes, but look here, my dear man, cut your
lengthy story short;

1. Literally 'lives on cold water and lye', a Norwegian expression for
destitution and neglect.

I've something altogether different weighing on my
    mind –
I've got myself in rather an uncomfortable position,
so that I need a statement, or perhaps an affidavit,
which, as my pa-in-law, you'd be well qualified to give.
– I'm sure that I could spare you a few coppers for a
    drink. . . .

THE OLD MAN: Well, well – so I can be of service to
    Your Highness?
Then, in return, I'd like to have a reference from *you*.

PEER GYNT: With pleasure. At the moment, money *is* a
    little scanty –
I'm having to economize in every way I can.
But let's come to the point: I expect you can remember
that evening I arrived up in the Rondë as a suitor –

THE OLD MAN:
Why, of course I can, Your Highness.

PEER GYNT:                    Let us do without
    the 'Highness'.
Well . . . you were proposing to do me an injury –
to damage my sight with a nick in the eyeball . . .
to turn me, in short, from Peer Gynt to a troll.
Now, what did I do? I resisted, remember?
– preferring to stand on my own two feet?
losing not only love, but position and power
simply and solely to stay as Myself –
and I want you to swear to that fact in the Courts.

THE OLD MAN:
Oh, I couldn't do that!

PEER GYNT:            What on earth do you mean?

THE OLD MAN: Well, you wouldn't expect me to perjure
    myself!
You surely remember you put on troll's breeches

and sampled our mead –

PEER GYNT:                     Well, I let you persuade me;
  but I flatly rejected the ultimate step,
  and that is what shows what a fellow is made of –
  it's the end of a song that you judge it by.

THE OLD MAN: But in fact, Peer, the end was the very
      reverse!

PEER GYNT: What nonsense is this?

THE OLD MAN:              When you went from the Rondë
  my motto was firmly engraved on your heart.

PEER GYNT: What motto?

THE OLD MAN:              That potent significant saying –

PEER GYNT:
  A saying?

THE OLD MAN: The one that distinguished humans
  from trolls, which is: 'Troll, to thyself be – enough!'

PEER GYNT [*recoiling a step*]: *Enough!*

THE OLD MAN:                  Yes, that's right; and
      from that day to this
  you've lived up to that motto as hard as you could!

PEER GYNT: *I* have? Peer Gynt?

THE OLD MAN [*weeping*]:          Yes, it's very ungrateful!
  You've lived as a troll, but you kept it a secret.
  The motto I taught you vouchsafed you the chance
  to go through the world as a man of some substance;
  and now you treat not only *me* with contempt,
  but also the motto you owe it all to!

PEER GYNT: 'Enough'! I – a hill troll? An Egoist? *I?*
  Well, it's perfectly clear that you *must* be mistaken!

THE OLD MAN [*producing a bundle of old newspapers*]:
  I suppose you imagine we don't have our papers!
  Just wait, and I'll show you, in red upon black,[1]

  1. Archer suggests that this is the trollish equivalent of 'in black and

how the *Brocken Gazette* has been singing your praises,
and the *Heklefjeld News* has been doing the same
from the very first winter you went overseas.
Just look at them, Peer; I'll willingly let you.
Here – this one's a leader signed 'Stallion's Hoof' –
and this 'On the National Spirit in Trolldom'.
The writer requests us to notice the fact
that the horns or the tail aren't what's really important
so long as the spirit's there under the skin.
'Our *Enough*', he concludes, 'gives the stamp of a troll
to a man,' quoting you as a perfect example.

PEER GYNT: But *I* – a hill-troll?

THE OLD MAN:                    Well, isn't it obvious?

PEER GYNT: So really I might have stayed just where I was,
and lived in the Rondë in comfort and peace,
and saved all that shoe-leather, trouble, and pains!
Peer Gynt a troll? Why, it's simply absurd!
Here's a farthing to get some tobacco. Good-bye.

THE OLD MAN: But my dear Prince Peer –

PEER GYNT:                    Go away – you're insane
or else senile! The right place for you is a Home!

THE OLD MAN: Ah, that's just exactly the thing that I want,
but my grandson's brats, as I told you just now,
have a great deal of influence here in these parts,
and they will insist that I'm only a fiction.
They *say* that one's own kith and kin are the worst,
and I, poor devil, am learning it's true.
It's hard when one only exists as a fable.

PEER GYNT: There are others, my dear man, who suffer
    from that![1]

---

white'. The Brocken (Blocksberg) and Heklefjeld were famous meeting-places for witches.

1. Peer, in the Auction scene, found that he, too, had become a legend.

THE OLD MAN: But among us trolls, there aren't any alms-boxes,

no Piggy-Banks, and no Charity Bonds . . .

such things would never catch on in the Rondë.

PEER GYNT: That's what comes of being 'Enough to yourselves'!

THE OLD MAN: Well, Your Highness can hardly complain of the saying . . .

and if you could help me in some way or other –

PEER GYNT: Now look here, my good man, you're on quite the wrong track;

I'm on my beam-ends,[1] as they call it, myself.

THE OLD MAN: Is that really the truth? Your Highness is broke?

PEER GYNT: Completely. My Highness is right in the red;

and it's all the fault of you cursèd trolls!

It just shows the result of bad company.

THE OLD MAN: So all my hopes have been dashed again!

I'd best make my way to the Town. Good-bye.

PEER GYNT: And when you get there . . .?

THE OLD MAN: I shall go on the stage;

They're advertising for National types.

PEER GYNT: Good luck to you, then; you can give them my love –

I'll be doing the same, once I get myself free.

I shall write them a farce, both absurd and profound,

and I'll call it *Sic Transit Gloria Mundi.*

[*He runs off down the path, leaving the* OLD MAN *calling after him.*]

\*

1. Literally 'on a bare hill'

*At a cross-roads.*

PEER GYNT: You're in trouble, Peer, now – as never before;

that trollish 'Enough' has pronounced your doom.

When your ship's on the rocks, you must cling to the wreckage!

*Anything* rather than go to the scrap-heap!

THE BUTTON MOULDER [*at the parting of the ways*]:

Well now, Peer Gynt, are your witnesses here?

PEER GYNT: The cross-roads already? You've not wasted time.

THE BUTTON MOULDER: I can see by your face, as plain as print,

what the answer is, before you tell me.

PEER GYNT: I'm tired of running ... one loses one's way. . . .

THE BUTTON MOULDER: Yes – and where does it lead to, after all?

PEER GYNT: True enough. And here in the forest at night –

THE BUTTON MOULDER: There's an old man trudging along – shall we call him?

PEER GYNT: No, leave him alone, my dear man, he's a drunkard.

THE BUTTON MOULDER:

But perhaps he could –

PEER GYNT:                    Sh! No, we'd best let him be.

THE BUTTON MOULDER:

Well then, shall we proceed?

PEER GYNT:                              I've just one question first:

what, after all, is this 'being one's self'?

THE BUTTON MOULDER: A curious question indeed, on
the lips
of a man who has just –

PEER GYNT: A direct answer, please.

THE BUTTON MOULDER: Being one's self means slaying
one's Self.
But that answer's presumably wasted on you,
and therefore let's say: 'Above everything else
it's observing the Master's intentions in all things.'

PEER GYNT: But what can one do if one's never found out
what the Master intended?

THE BUTTON MOULDER: One just has to guess.

PEER GYNT: But a man's intuitions so often prove wrong,
and then one is sunk,[1] as it were, in mid-ocean!

THE BUTTON MOULDER: Exactly, Peer Gynt, it's when
insight is lacking
that the lad with the hoof makes the best of his
captures.

PEER GYNT: It all seems a most controversial point. . . .
Look – I'll give up my claim to have been myself –
since it well might turn out not too easy to prove,
I'll write off that part of my case as a loss.
But just now, as I wandered alone on the moor,
my conscience was pinching me just like a shoe,
and I said to myself: 'After all, you're a sinner –!'

THE BUTTON MOULDER: But now you've come back to
the point where we started.

PEER GYNT: No, no, not at all; I contend I'm a *great*
one –
not only in deed, but in thought and in word.
I led a most dissolute life when abroad!

1. This is *ad undas* in the original, but Latin phrases are not so familiar in
England today as perhaps they were in nineteenth-century Norway.

THE BUTTON MOULDER: That's as may be; but what
    can you show me to prove it?

PEER GYNT: Well, just give me time and I'll look for a
    priest;
 I'll confess to him quickly, and bring you his statement.

THE BUTTON MOULDER: Yes, do that if you can, it
    might well clear things up,
 and then you'd be saved from the casting-ladle;
 but my orders, Peer Gynt –

PEER GYNT:            They're on very old paper –
 they certainly date from a long time ago ...
 from the days when I lived a most scandalous life,
 and posed as a prophet and trusted to fate.
 Well, may I just try it?

THE BUTTON MOULDER: But –

PEER GYNT:              Be a good fellow –
 you surely can't have very much on your hands,
 for the air in this part of the country's so healthy
 it adds year upon year on to everyone's life.
 Don't forget what the Pastor at Justedal[1] wrote:
 'It's seldom that anyone dies in this valley.'

THE BUTTON MOULDER: As far as the next cross-roads,
    then – but no farther.

PEER GYNT: A priest! If I have to catch him by force!
    [*He runs off.*]

\*

*A heathery slope, with a path winding on upwards over
the hill.*

PEER GYNT: There are one or two ways that this might
    come in handy –

1. Matthias Fosse wrote a description of his parish of Justedal in 1750.
There was an early unfinished play by Ibsen: *The White Grouse of Justedal.*

as Esben said, finding a magpie's wing.[1]
Who would have thought that, so late in the day,
a sinful life might preserve one's skin?
Yes, things were becoming a little bit ticklish,
it was out of the frying-pan into the fire.[2]
It all goes to show that the proverb is right
when it says that wherever there's life there's hope.

> [A THIN PERSON *in a cassock well tucked up, and*
> *carrying a fowling-net over his shoulder, comes*
> *running down the slope.*]

PEER GYNT: Who's this? A priest with a fowling-net?
Hurray, then I've really got luck on my side!
Good evening, Herr Pastor. The path's rather rough –

THE THIN ONE:
But one puts up with much for the sake of a soul!

PEER GYNT:
Ah, so somebody's bound for heaven, then?

THE THIN ONE:                                No –
I hope that he's going the opposite way.

PEER GYNT: May I walk with you, Herr Pastor, a little?

THE THIN ONE: With pleasure, some company's just what
I'd like.

PEER GYNT: I've a weight on my mind –

THE THIN ONE:                    Then out with it, man!

PEER GYNT: You look as if you're a reliable chap.
Now, I've carefully kept all the laws of the land,
and I've never been put under lock and key. . . .
But from time to time a man loses his footing
and stumbles –

THE THIN ONE: Ah, even the best of us!

---

1. In the fairy-tale, Esben Askeladd picked up a magpie's wing, and the
adventures that followed led him to a bride and a kingdom.
2. The Norwegian equivalent is 'out of the ashes into the flames.'

PEER GYNT:                                    Yes –
and these trifles –

THE THIN ONE:    They *were* only trifles?

PEER GYNT:                                    Of course,
I've never indulged in more grandiose sinning.

THE THIN ONE: Then please, my dear man, don't come
          bothering *me* –
I'm not quite the person you seem to imagine.
Take a look at my fingers – well, how do they strike
          you?

PEER GYNT: Your nails are uncommonly over-developed.

THE THIN ONE: What else? Ah, you're stealing a glance
          at my foot.

PEER GYNT [*pointing*]: Is that a real hoof?

THE THIN ONE:                       So I'm happy to think.

PEER GYNT [*raising his hat*]: I'd have taken my oath on it
          you were a parson!
And so I've the honour –? Well, so much the better.
When the front door stands open, you don't use the
          back one!
When you meet with the king, you can disregard
          lackeys!

THE THIN ONE: You seem an unprejudiced fellow – shake
          hands!
Well, my friend, in what way am I able to help
          you?
You mustn't go asking for wealth or for power,
I'll be hanged if I'm able to give such things these days;
you wouldn't believe how bad business is,
the bottom has fallen right out of the market –
one just can't get souls – except one at a time
now and then –

PEER GYNT:    Is mankind so reformed?

THE THIN ONE: On the contrary, men have deteriorated
   till most of them end in the casting-ladle.
PEER GYNT: Ah yes, I've been hearing a bit about that –
   in fact, *that*'s just the thing that I've come here about.
THE THIN ONE: Speak freely.
PEER GYNT:                        Well, if it's not *too* much to ask,
   I should very much like –
THE THIN ONE:                        Board and lodging, perhaps?
PEER GYNT: You've guessed what I want before ever I
      asked you!
   You've told me yourself that your business is bad,
   so it wouldn't perhaps be too much of a favour –
THE THIN ONE: My dear sir –
PEER GYNT:                        I'm not really asking for much,
   I shouldn't expect you to pay me a salary –
   just a friendly arrangement to suit the conditions.
THE THIN ONE:
   A warm room?
PEER GYNT:         Not *too* warm! And – this is essential –
   permission to leave again, freely and openly . . .
   the right, as they say, to go back on my tracks
   if it looks as if better things might be ahead.
THE THIN ONE: My friend, I am really exceedingly sorry
   but you'd never believe what a lot of requests,
   on those very same lines, I keep getting from clients
   when they're leaving the scene of their earthly en-
      deavours.
PEER GYNT: But when you consider the things that I've
      done,
   I'm exactly the kind that you seem to be seeking –
THE THIN ONE:
   But you said they were trifles!
PEER GYNT:                        Perhaps, in a sense.

Though, now I remember, I trafficked in slaves!

THE THIN ONE: There are those who have trafficked in
    minds and in souls,
in a trivial way – but they didn't get in.

PEER GYNT: I exported a number of idols to China –

THE THIN ONE: Mere hucksters' talk! We laugh at such
    things;
there are people exporting much uglier idols
in sermons, in literature, and in art,
yet *they* don't get in.

PEER GYNT:        Ah, but listen to this:
I once went and passed myself off as a Prophet!

THE THIN ONE: What – abroad? Why, that's nothing!
    Such casual sinning[1]
is certain to end in the casting-ladle.
If you've nothing better to back your claim,
as much as I'd like to, I can't take you in.

PEER GYNT: Well, when I was shipwrecked, I sat on a
    keel
and stayed there – a drowning man clings to a straw,
and they also say: 'Every man for himself' . . .
so I more or less robbed the Cook of his life!

THE THIN ONE: I'd be better pleased if you'd 'more or
    less'
robbed a kitchen-maid of something else!
What is all this prattle of 'more or less'?
Now, I ask you, who do you think would waste
expensive fuel – and in these hard times –
on such half-hearted rubbish as that?

---

1. Ibsen uses a German phrase; the line runs 'Most people's *Seen ins*
*Blaue* ends in the casting ladle.' Archer takes *Seen* to be a misspelling of
*sehen*, but as Ibsen starts the word with a capital letter, he must have meant
it as a noun.

Now don't get upset – it's your sins I'm belittling
not you – so excuse me for speaking so bluntly.
But look, my dear friend, just give up the idea,[1]
and get used to the thought of the casting-ladle.
Would it really help if I boarded and lodged you?
Just consider – you seem quite a rational man.
Oh, I freely admit that your memory's good,
but a bird's eye view of all you recall
is only, however you look at it,
what a Frenchman[2] might label '*Pas grand'chose*'.
You have nothing either to howl for or smile at,
nothing either to cheer or despair about,
nothing to make you turn hot and cold . . .
merely some things that might vex you a little!

PEER GYNT: They do say there's no way to tell where the
   shoe
will pinch you, except by trying it on.

THE THIN ONE:
Quite true. Though I – thanks to So-and-so –
don't need any more than one odd boot.
But it's lucky we've touched on the subject of boots,
it reminds me I'd better be getting along;
I've a joint to collect which I hope will prove fat,
so I haven't the time to stand gossiping here.

PEER GYNT: And might I inquire on what diet of sin
   this fellow was nourished?

THE THIN ONE:                     As far as I know,
he has just been Himself all the days of his life,
and that, after all, is the one thing that matters.

---

1. Literally 'knock out that tooth'.
2. In the original it is a Swede and the phrase is *bra litet rolig* (very poor sport). It would be as well understood in Norway as would *pas grand'chose* in England.

PEER GYNT: Himself? Does your realm take in people like
that?

THE THIN ONE: That depends – but the door is at least
left ajar.
Remember, a man may quite well be Himself
in two different ways – he could be, as it were,
the inside or outside face of the garment.
You know that in Paris they've lately discovered
a way to take portraits by means of the sun.
There is either a picture that's faithful to life,
or else what is known as a 'negative'.
The latter reverses the black and the white
and looks hideous, seen by the casual eye,
but all the same, the likeness is there,
and all that it needs is bringing out.
So if, in the course of its life, a soul
has remained a negative photograph,
they don't, for that reason, destroy the plate –
they send it, just as it is, to me,
and I set about to complete the process
and develop the thing by appropriate means.
I steam it, I soak it, I burn it, I clean it
in liquid sulphur, and such-like ingredients,
till the picture that *should* have been there appears
as what is known as 'a positive'.
But when, as in your case, it's almost rubbed off,
neither sulphur nor alkali helps in the least.

PEER GYNT: So a man may come down to you black as a
crow
and depart like a swan . . .?[1] Might I ask you the name
of this 'negative image' you told me about

[1]. Literally 'a grouse in winter plumage', but that hardly strikes us
immediately as a symbol of whiteness.

whom you hope to convert to a positive?

THE THIN ONE: The name's Peter Gynt.

PEER GYNT: Peter Gynt? Oh indeed?
Now, is Herr Gynt Himself?

THE THIN ONE: He maintains that he is.

PEER GYNT: Well, the said Herr Peter's [1] a trustworthy
fellow.

THE THIN ONE:
You know him, perhaps?

PEER GYNT: Yes, I do – in a way;
but one knows lots of people. . . .

THE THIN ONE: I haven't much time –
so where last did you see him?

PEER GYNT: Oh – down at the Cape.

THE THIN ONE:
Of Good Hope? [2]

PEER GYNT: Yes, that's right. But unless I'm mis-
taken
he was just on the point of sailing away.

THE THIN ONE: Then I'd better get down there as fast as
I can,
I only hope I shall catch him in time.
The Cape, eh? I've never cared much for the Cape –
one keeps meeting missionaries there from Stavanger! [3]
[*He goes off southwards.*]

PEER GYNT: The stupid creature – he's off at a bound
with his tongue hanging out. Well, he'll find he's been
hoaxed!
It was fun to be able to hoodwink him so –

---

1. So in the original, though Ibsen first wrote 'Peer'.

2. This is *Di Buona Speranza* in the original. Though Ibsen was writing
in Italy, there seems little reason for using Italian.

3. The home of the Norwegian Missionary Society.

he was so overbearing and put on such airs!
Yet he hadn't so much to be uppish about –
he'll hardly get fat in his present profession,
he'll probably soon be turned out, neck and crop.
Hm . . . *I'm* not too firm in the saddle myself,
I'm expelled, you might say, from the *Self*-owning
        class !¹

>        [*A shooting-star shines out – he bows to it.*]

A salute from Peer Gynt, Brother Shooting-star!
Shine out – then fade . . . and be lost in the void. . . .

>        [*He collects himself nervously and goes deeper into the*
>        *mist. After a moment's silence, he cries out*]

Is there no one? No one in all creation?
No one on earth and no one in heaven . . .?

>        [*He comes out farther down, throws his hat on the*
>        *ground and tears his hair. After a while, he becomes*
>        *quieter.*]

So unspeakably poor can the soul return
through the sombre mists into nothingness.
Do not be angry, oh lovely earth,
if, to no purpose, I trampled your grass.
Oh lovely sun, your glowing rays
have squandered themselves on an empty house
where no one within might be warmed and gladdened –
the owner, they say, was never at home.
Lovely sun and lovely earth,
you were foolish to warm and nourish my mother.
How lavish is Nature, how mean is the spirit;
how dearly man pays for his birth, with his life.
I will climb up high to the steepest peak
and watch the sun rise once again;

1. Literally 'the Self-owning nobility'. *Selvejer* is the normal word for
'freeholder'.

I will stare till I tire, at the promised land,
then let the snow drift over me. . . .
And there they may write: 'Here lies – No One.'
and after . . . after . . . let come what may.

CHURCHGOERS [*singing on the forest path*]:
> Blessèd Morn when God's word came
> Down to earth in tongues of flame;
> Since that day, God's heirs have sung
> Praise to Him in Heaven's own tongue.

PEER GYNT [*shrinking with fear*]: I will not look! *There* is
desert and waste.

I fear I was dead before I die.

> [*He tries to slink away into the bushes, but finds
> himself at the cross-roads.*]

THE BUTTON MOULDER: Good morning, Peer Gynt. The
list of your sins?

PEER GYNT: Do you think that I haven't whistled and
called
as hard as I could?

THE BUTTON MOULDER: And nobody came?

PEER GYNT: No one at all but a roving photographer.

THE BUTTON MOULDER: Well, time is up.

PEER GYNT:                                                 Then all is up!
The owl smells the dawn – can you hear him hooting?

THE BUTTON MOULDER: That's the Mattins bell . . .

PEER GYNT:                                         What is that shining?

THE BUTTON MOULDER: Only a light in the hut.

PEER GYNT:                                               And that sighing?

THE BUTTON MOULDER: Only a woman's song.

PEER GYNT:                                             There – *there* I shall find
the list of my sins!

THE BUTTON MOULDER [*taking hold of him*]:
> Set your house in order.

[*They have come out of the wood, and are standing in front of the hut. It is dawn.*]

PEER GYNT: Set my house in order? It's *here*. Now go!
Be off! Were your ladle as big as a coffin
be assured it could not hold me and my sins!

THE BUTTON MOULDER: Till the *third* cross-roads then,
Peer. But there . . .!
[*He turns away and goes.*]

PEER GYNT [*approaching the hut*]:
Backwards or forwards, it's just as far.
Out or in, it's just as narrow.
[*He stops.*]
No! Like a wild unceasing lament
*some*thing bids me go in . . . go back – go home.
[*He goes a few paces, but stops again.*]
'Round about' said the Boyg!
[*He hears the song in the hut.*]
                                    No! Now for once
the way runs straight, though it's never so narrow.
[*He runs towards the hut, but at that moment*
SOLVEIG *comes out of the door. She is dressed for
church, and she has her prayerbook in her hand-
kerchief. She walks with a stick.*[1] *She stands for a
moment, upright and gentle.*]

PEER GYNT [*throwing himself down at the threshold*]:
If you'd judge a sinner, then speak out now!

SOLVEIG: It is he – it is he! Oh, praise be to God.
[*She feels for him.*]

PEER GYNT: Cry aloud how sinfully I have offended!

SOLVEIG: You have sinned in nothing, my only
love.

---

1. Because she is nearly blind.

[*She gropes for him again, and finds him.*]

**THE BUTTON MOULDER** [*behind the hut*]:

The list, Peer Gynt.

**PEER GYNT:** Call out my crimes!

**SOLVEIG** [*sitting down beside him*]: You have made my life a
beautiful song.

Blest may you be that you come at last –

blest that we meet at Pentecost.

**PEER GYNT:** Then I am lost.

**SOLVEIG:** There is One who will save.

**PEER GYNT** [*with a laugh*]: Lost! . . . Unless you can solve
a riddle.

**SOLVEIG:** What is it?

**PEER GYNT:** What is it? Ah yes – of course:

Where has Peer Gynt been since last we met?

**SOLVEIG:** Where?

**PEER GYNT:** With his destiny on his brow.

Where? Since he sprang from the mind of God?

Can you tell me that? If you cannot tell,

I must go down to the shadowy land.

**SOLVEIG** [*smiling*]: Oh, your riddle is easy.

**PEER GYNT:** Then say, if you know!

Where was I? Myself – complete and whole?

Where? With God's seal upon my brow?

**SOLVEIG:** In my faith, in my hope, and in my love.

**PEER GYNT** [*recoiling with a start*]:

What are you saying? You juggle with words;

you are mother yourself to the lad who is there.

**SOLVEIG:** I am – I am! But who is his father?

It is He who forgives when a mother prays.

**PEER GYNT** [*his face lights up, and he cries out*]:

My mother – my wife! Oh, purest of women –

hide me, oh hide me, within your love.

[*He clings to her tightly, burying his face in her lap.
There is a long silence. The sun rises.*]

SOLVEIG [*singing softly*]:
Sleep now, dearest son of mine,
I will cradle you, I will guard you.

Child, you have nestled on your mother's knee [1]
we two have been playing all the livelong day.

Child, you have lingered at your mother's breast
all the livelong day. God bless you, my joy.

Child, I have held you close against my breast
all the livelong day. You are weary now.

Sleep now, dearest son of mine,
I will cradle you, I will guard you.

THE BUTTON MOULDER'S VOICE [*behind the hut*]:
Peer, we shall meet at the last cross-roads,
and then we shall see if . . . I'll say no more.

SOLVEIG [*singing more loudly in the sunshine*]:
I will cradle you, I will guard you;
sleep and dream, dearest son of mine.

1. In these last three couplets, Ibsen makes Solveig suddenly
address him in the third person. In English it is more natural to
keep to the second person; also it fits Grieg's music better.